RETIRED, REWIRED

Living Without Adult Supervision in Bali

Cat Wheeler

TOKAY
PRESS

Retired, Rewired
Published by CV. Bayu Graphic

Copyright 2016 by Catherine Wheeler, Indonesia

All rights reserved. No part of this book may be produced or transmitted in any manner whatsoever without the prior written permission of the Publisher, except by a reviewer who may quote brief passages in a review.

ISBN: 978-152-04644-2-8

Cover and page layout by Bayugraphic, Denpasar

Back cover photo by J. Bigio

For Jenny, dear friend and co-adventuress through many journeys over many years. Without your support, vision, love, direction and occasional well-timed bossiness my books would not exist and I would be a very different person.

Retired, Rewired

This isn't a book about the nuts and bolts of living in Bali as a retiree. It's a random collection of thoughts and experiences over the 16 years I've been growing older here, in no particular order. I think of my life in Bali as a sitcom with an ever changing cast of people and animals and a very unpredictable script. Some stories explore lifestyle options going forward, since I anticipate I'll be dying here. And there's going to be quite a lot of going forward, because my DNA indicates the likelihood another three decades or so of living without adult supervision.

I first came to Ubud in 1969 as a teenager. My family was based in Malaysia and I travelled to Java and Bali with two friends during the school holidays. Indonesia was not very tourist-friendly in those days, and we had some adventures. In retrospect, my parents were amazingly naïve to allow us to make that journey. We not only survived unscathed, but I came back with a trove of memories that stayed with me for decades. Little did I realise that I would return 30 years later and spend what will probably be the latter half of my life here.

People sometimes say, "You live in Bali! You're so lucky!" Actually, luck had very little to with it. Creating a life here involved hard decisions, some courage and most of my savings. It was like stepping off a cliff and free-falling into the unknown... then landing, not only on my feet, but in a magical tropical garden.

When I was incubating this book I asked some of the retired community here what 'retirement' in the context of Bali meant to them. The words freedom, time and choice kept coming up. We can stretch, observe, experiment. Several people mentioned that they felt they'd been re-wired.

Rewired, recalibrated, redefined. Free-falling into place in Bali.

Cat Wheeler
November 2016

INDEX

Retired, Rewired iv
Redefining Retirement 1
Living Without
Adult Supervision 4
Growing Old Disgracefully 8
Behind Closed (Refrigerator) Doors 12
In Darkest Domestica 16
Every Second Wednesday 20
Animal Days 23
In Celebration of the Simple Life 27
It Wasn't Always
Like This 31
There's Something About Hamish 34
A Table's Tale 38
Eat Pray Freeze – from Ubud to Umbria 42
Gambols with Gastropods 47
The Turn of
the Wheel 51
The Lighter Side of Urban Development 54
Only in Ubud 58
Changing Times 62
Stormy Weather 66
The Real Ubud Community 70
Definitely and Absolutely the
Last House 74
A House in Bali 78
Stranger in a
Strange Land 84
A Lesson in Cherishing 89

- Bring on the Dancing Girls ... 93
- The Smallest Room ... 98
- Pig Tales ... 101
- The Geography of Loss ... 106
- On the Carpet ... 110
- Talking to Tokays ... 114
- Bali Behind the Seen ... 118
- Gone to the Dogs ... 122
- Ubud, the One-Trick Pony ... 126
- The Art of Happiness, Bali-Style ... 130
- Nobody Likes a Mean Duck ... 134
- Havoc in the Henhouse ... 138
- Mildred's Last Egg ... 146
- Along Came a Spider ... 149
- Losing the Plot in Paradise ... 154
- The Last Lap ... 158

Redefining Retirement

Having just turned 65, I'm taking an anthropological interest in the distinct disconnect between what we were brought up expecting retirement to be and the lives we're living now. When I was young people expected to be old at 70, so they became old. These days my friends in their 70s are bouncy, healthy, interested and interesting.

Technically, I am retired. That's what my visa says, and I receive a modest old age pension. But we need a new word for whatever it is we're doing. The old definition of 'to leave your job or stop working because of old age or ill health' emphatically does not apply to the increasing number of mature foreigners living here.

The concept of retirement is a fairly new one. Until a century or so ago people didn't live as long and pensions were rare, so most folk worked until they dropped. Germany was the first country to introduce retirement in 1889. But these days, especially in developed countries, people are living longer and healthier lives. By the time they reach official retirement age (between 65 and 68 in most countries) they - I mean, we -may have a quarter of their lives still ahead of us.

Our cultures and economies dismiss us after we cross this arbitrary line in the sand. We become invisible except as a new market for cruises and adult nappies. Indonesia considers people over 60 so decrepit that they may no longer donate blood. Only slowly are the rule-makers and marketers becoming aware that ours is the generation that discovered sex, drugs, rock and roll, yoga, health food, civil disobedience and quite a lot more, and we are still engaged. Our hair may be silver now, but we are not about to sit down and quietly get old. Not while there still distant places to visit, new cuisines to sample and tales to tell.

When I moved from Singapore in 2000, Ubud wasn't remotely a retirement destination. The limited rental housing stock and facilities for retirees at that time were in the south. Only about 2010 did the major shift begin with elders moving to Bali. Now there are significant numbers of us navigating the Byzantine, ever-shifting immigration regulations and sharing the names of the good doctors who can mend our cataracts, give us new hips and knees and maybe pop in a stent or two.

The Bali government has been wondering how to optimize retirement tourism. The initial plan was to create retirement communities within traditional Balinese villages, which presents some mind-boggling issues of cross-cultural integration and disparate standards of living. Now the focus is on establishing free standing retirement communities in several locations. In order for this concept to fly the authorities will have to make it more straightforward to obtain retirement visas and improve health care to international standards. That will be nice.

Living in Bali has a Zen-like quality that keeps reeling us back to the present moment. We come from our other lives with the habit of multi-tasking and long term planning. But the Balinese live very much in the present. Many don't multi-task at all well, and become stressed when required to. Our lives here tend to lack routine, and those who try to cling to routine can be sure that Bali will disrupt it. Plans have a way of shape-shifting, appearing and disappearing like incense smoke. (My own strict routine is to wake up, pee, brush my teeth and it's chaos from then on.)

Add to this the nature of land laws here which dictate that we can't own property. So we live within our current lease however long that may be, and don't plan ahead for future generations. Then there's the factor of paying the whole lease in advance, a significant commitment of cash and faith in a country where the goal posts keep moving. It all keeps us just a little bit off balance and less attached to predictable outcomes, so we never become bored. Quite the contrary. Managing even small projects here can be very stimulating.

Besides having the time to paint, write, dance, trek, sing and perform community service we now have time to watch the garden grow. We ponder the imponderable. And people in our communities begin inevitably to decline. They fall down and break things, they develop dementia, they die. We have to learn to cope with these misadventures, within the context of a different culture with different rules.

But apart from the grim stuff, life in Bali is a blessing for the rewired. We're not only free of having to work for a living, but we're also free of our society's expectations of people our age. So many of us are clinically eccentric that it's become the new normal.

Living Without Adult Supervision

Life has been building up to warp speed over the past couple of decades. All the modern conveniences that were supposed to free us up for more leisure have actually made us more frantic. Email, devices, fitness regimes and self-improvement courses fill our days. Everything has gotten faster, from yoga to wifi (though not on my street). We are multi-tasking like never before.

It's exhausting.

When I fled the rat-race of Singapore for then-sleepy Ubud in 2000, I already knew there was nowhere on earth quite like this droll little town with its strong sense of self and its gritty charm. Ubud has taken years to reveal its mother lode of accomplished escapees to me. The corporate refugees are legion. Tax lawyers. Computer wizards. Consultants of every flavour. Executives. News producers. Chefs. Psychologists. Designers. Teachers. Managers. Artists. Publishers. They are all here, and many more, concealed in snug cottages overlooking rice fields and lush jungle. Many of them came to Ubud for two weeks -- ten years ago. The rest, as they say, is history.

Moving from the strict adult supervision of Singapore to the spontaneous chaos of Bali was a revelation. The Balinese had plenty of rules for themselves but very few for us. We were light years outside of their ken on almost every dimension, and I believe they found us vastly entertaining. (I wrote this piece several years ago, and fear that this is probably no longer true).

Ubud conceals a particularly agreeable sub-species of expatriate. These people cut the cord to their countries of birth decades ago to embrace life abroad without adult supervision with delight, curiosity and gratitude. Aged between 65 and 90, to a man and a woman they are intelligent, funny, accomplished, eccentric, life-affirming and highly respectful of the culture in which they live. My favourites just happen to be animal lovers and gardeners who enjoy good food and exotic cocktails.

We don't talk very often about what we did in the Other Life. Sometimes we try to remember when we last wore a suit or attended a meeting in a room without windows. We agree that there were far too many of those. It used to be routine to drive an hour or more in each direction to an office or a restaurant, or to deal with junk mail... remember getting actual mail? We attended too many cocktail parties in high heeled shoes, breathed the fumes of two-hour traffic jams and lugged heavy briefcases around for 12 hours a day, on and off airplanes and into soulless, air-conditioned office blocks.

That was then. This is now.

We are the ones that got away. The ones who came to the edge one day in New York or London or Bangkok and heard a muted gamelan beyond the urban chaos. Saw the shimmer of a rice field in the rear view mirror of a car stuck in an endless traffic jam. Sensed a simpler, more contented life. Dropped the briefcase and walked away.

Chasing a bat out of the bathroom of my simple cottage, I occasionally remember the years of five-star hotels with their vast, batless marble bathrooms. Sometimes I get calls from friends who are still lugging the briefcase; they ask, "What's that noise?" I explain that it's a priest chanting prayers across the river in the dark, or frogs having an orgy in my pond. They don't think I'm so crazy anymore. My guestroom has become a sanctuary for burned-out executives from Singapore and Sydney.

I used to volunteer in the Smile Shop, a little second hand store in Ubud that raised money for facial deformity surgery. Arriving for my shift one Sunday morning I found a large plastic bag hanging on the door handle. Inside were two neatly folded women's suits and several pairs of pumps, nearly new. Another refugee from the corporate world.

The ex-tax lawyer now reads tarot cards and the ex-news producer has taken up photography and practices yoga. People wear comfy shoes. Almost everybody has a favourite community project, does volunteer work or is putting a local kid or two through school. Some of us have embraced the simpler life to a point that a visit to Ace Hardware is an exciting day out.

I met them slowly, over time, because most of these people are card-carrying introverts. They consider a group of eight people to be the extreme limit of a social event. That means lots of events, because they have many friends. A few of them are not introverts, and enquire why we have three dinner parties for six people instead of one big free-for-all. We can't answer.

According to the Indonesian government, people over the age of 60 are technically geriatric. But doddering as we are, we still we manage to enjoy a rich social life.

When introverted geriatrics party, we start at about four in the afternoon. Because most of us like to be in bed early, we have to work backwards from bedtime. We always have a driver, of course, because often these festivities take place in a distant banjar and there will be cocktails.

The driveway of the house to which we are headed is long and steep, curving down through a virtual botanic garden of rare plants. Unless it's pouring with rain we park at the top and take our time ambling down it, admiring the landscaping and drinking in the vista of forests and rice fields. If the weather is fine, a bright display of rainbow penjors has been raised to greet us. Our host often meets us halfway to the house, pulling wine glasses and a bottle of chilled wine from beneath a handy bush.

While we sip the wine and wander past the quail, lovebirds and ducks, the dogs discover us and gallop up for a greeting. The largest is a sweet, unlovely French bulldog scarred by an encounter with a cobra, who escorts us safely past the geese that guard the front door.

Once inside, the other few guests have already assembled, and are noisily laying out the meal. On this occasion we will lounge around (there is no dining table in this establishment) a selection of fine fresh cheeses, one of them very smelly indeed, with nuts and chutney on the side. The main course is a huge bowl of sensational mashed potatoes, seasoned with much spirited philosophical discussion. For dessert we share a bar of fine chocolate with bacon in it.

"Maybe we do need adult supervision," muses one member of the party, observing that several essential food groups seemed to be missing from our menu. She was shouted down as the port was poured.

We began to yawn as the light faded. The chef curled up for a nap, surrounded by elderly dogs. The host looked pointedly at his watch; it was 7:30. Happy and sleepy, we wandered up to the car and were delivered home just in time for bed. In fact, we are routinely taking off our party clothes about the time same time the sophisticates of Seminyak are donning theirs.

It's a good thing our mothers don't know what we get up to.

Growing Old Disgracefully

There's a lot more grey hair on the streets of Ubud these days. Ours.

Increasing numbers of expats are retiring to Bali, and those of us who have been here for years are firmly rooted and not planning to go anywhere. But costs keep rising, our small fixed incomes are eroded by global economic dramas and we keep getting older, somehow.

I look at the situation in the west, where the fastest-growing demographic is the elderly. Only now are governments starting to realize that this population has unique housing and care needs. When my father had a stroke in Vancouver, every bed on his hospital ward held an elder. The emergency room was full of people over 80. In western countries, many elders live alone. They forget their medication. It's hard to shop for food, and to cook and do laundry. They fall down a lot. They're lonely. It's pretty depressing, thinking about growing old in the west. If I'm going to get old (not negotiable) and fall down I want to do it right here where Wayan Manis will pick me up, dust me off and make me a cup of tea, thank you very much.

People in western cultures discuss everything these days except death. Dying is the last taboo. People seem to think that if they don't talk about it, it won't happen. Gentle reader, it is going to happen. We're all going to die. And before that, we're probably going to live long enough to get old.

A circle of friends in Ubud has been mulling this over for years now, thinking about the future and our eventual graceful fall off the perch. There's a lot to be said for growing old in the company of friends, both expat and Balinese, in a place where the hearts around us are as warm as the morning garden in January. We want to stay here. We're happy here. In decades to come we can totter around together and bitch about our arthritis. And communities of elder expats are good for the local economy. Most of our rupiah end up in our Balinese neighbours' pockets as we pay for rent, staff salaries, groceries, restaurant meals and transportation.

Retirement visas make it legally possible to finish our lives in Bali, but we need to start creating resources for our older selves now. Affordable housing is one of the biggest concerns. For years we've been talking about forming small communities as we grew older, maybe renovating an old home stay or small hotel. We planned to have our own modest rooms or cottages but share staff, caregivers, a vehicle, library and (if this absurd alcohol situation remains unresolved) a still. The real estate boom has put this concept beyond the reach of most of us, so we're exploring other options. A few years ago I went into the development business in a very small way, and it opened my eyes to an empty niche in the local housing market.

My staff told me that there was a shell of a building on a bit of land next to their compound in Singakerta they were thinking of turning into a kos (rooms for cheap monthly rental to other Indonesians). I went to have a look. It was pretty dire -- two small dark rooms opening to the outside, no real loo and a cave of a kitchen without running water. A flex from the compound next door lit a couple of five watt light bulbs. We measured it up and I went home to have a think and make a drawing. The next day I offered to lend the family the money to finish the building to modest western standards according to my design.

It was an educational and entertaining project for all of us. I wanted to keep the expenditure as low as possible to minimize their debt load which meant researching local and recycled materials. Nyoman had to learn to upgrade his building skills and embrace concepts like a big septic cistern, new water tank and an independent electrical supply. He raised the ceiling, blocked up one of the room doors to the outside and opened the wall between the two interior rooms. I encouraged him to replace the shiny white floor tile and punch out more windows for light.

The design touches were fun; we found old-fashioned tinted cement tiles at a good price, and a little granite sink for the bathroom for the same cost as a ceramic one. Nyoman plastered, painted, made a patio in the front with a built-in day bed and carved a handsome wooden front door. The little house, now inviting and fresh, took him about 3 months to finish. The family owns the wee bit land it stands on, Nyoman contributed the labour and I lent them the money for the materials. The house paid for itself within a year. Now they have an asset bringing regular income to the family for the foreseeable future and I have another option to move into when my contract runs out in Tebesaya.

There's not much for rent at that price point in Ubud these days, and as the expat population ages people are going to be seeking small, one-level, secure and affordable houses. I started to look around and saw that plenty of families had enough empty non-agricultural land to build an independent little house for rent. These are not villas, they are granny flats. They can be simple, but must be safe and accessible for the elderly without stairs or slippery, shiny floors and with wide doorways to accommodate wheelchairs or walkers. These small homes (I'm talking about 50 square metres here) are astonishingly cheap to build, using local or recycled materials. It makes sense to start building up housing stock for this market now, and helping our Balinese neighbours create assets for the future. Clusters of them in the same neighbourhood would be a good idea, as it would allow friends to live in communities.

After affordable accommodation, we're going to need carers. Our circle of friends includes one member who is in frail health and sometimes requires home care, and two who have Alzheimer's. We've already learned that the Balinese make wonderful caregivers, and several have been trained in home care, dementia management and occupational therapy skills. These carers will be able to make periodic or daily home visits or live in according to the elders' needs. Maybe we'll train them to operate the still as well.

Just because we're old doesn't mean we have to stop partying.

Then there's the last leg. Until recently, expats who passed away in Bali had to be dispatched at a hideous crematorium on the Bukit. Many of us have sent off friends or acquaintances there over the years, mourning not only their departure but the singularly depressing environment in which the deed was done. After living out one's life in one of the world's most lovely places and complex cultures, it's incongruous to end up in what more than one observer has called the Pizza Oven. We continue to seek alternatives.

One of our friends with Alzheimer's lived in the little house we built in Singakerta with his devoted carers. The people of the village accepted his eccentricities and the neighbours sent over fried bananas whenever they made a batch. He was our ambassador, in a way -- the first of us to live in the village as a dependent elder. As the years go by we will follow, and eventually become part of the soil of this island we love so much.

Behind Closed (Refrigerator) Doors

One evening a few weeks ago a friend casually opened my freezer in search of some ice to cool her drink, only to find the entire compartment full of small bags of frozen dark red liquid.

"Mulberry juice?" she hazarded.

Ummm… actually, no. Blood.

No, I have not resorted to vampirism. I hardly ever even eat red meat. The blood was a gift from a friend who has a business in free range chickens, and sometimes brings me a bag after he processes his birds for sale. Cooked with red rice and vegetables, blood is excellent dog food.

But this is not a story about canine nutrition. The incident made me realize how easy it is to appear to be slipping over the edge of charming eccentricity into downright barminess. I mean, blood is pure protein, it's a natural food free of chemicals and the dogs thrive on it, so isn't it logical to keep a few bags in the freezer? But to someone straight off the plane from Sydney with a bottle of Bombay Sapphire under her arm, it was rather bizarre.

I'm often asked by readers why so many of my stories seem to be about the animals in my life and people seldom appear on stage. There's a very good reason for this. Ubud is full of delightful eccentrics, most of them expats. (Well, many of them are delightful. Some are less so. And the ones who aren't eccentric are much less interesting.) If I was given to works of fiction, it would be very tempting to populate a novel with thinly veiled characters from the shattered sidewalks, yoga shalas and colonic studios of Ubud. But even if I changed names, ages, nationalities and even genders, they would be instantly recognizable to themselves and others in the community. If I wrote about the expats in Ubud, I'd have to leave town.

So instead of writing about personalities, I'm going to focus on their refrigerators. Many folk who would pass for normal if encountered on the streets of Ubud in broad daylight have been known to secrete some very unusual things in their refrigerators. Granted that these are the tropics and a cooler ambience is required for some items such as vitamins and expensive cosmetics. But even I was surprised at the wide variety of articles to be found behind those closed refrigerator doors. Just for the record, I did not make any of this up.

Margie and her husband have spent much of the year in Ubud since the 1980s and the balance of the time at their home in Oregon. When I wrote this, their daughter had delivered a son there two years previously. I learned that Margie's grandson's placenta is still in her freezer in Eugene. "I guess we should bury it," she said recently. They often have a friend staying at their Oregon house while they're in Bali. Was the placenta in the freezer labeled? I wondered. "No," she said thoughtfully. "And I told him to eat whatever he found in the fridge." We both mulled over the scenario of the current house sitter opening the freezer door at a hungry moment and spotting the unidentified bag... "We should definitely bury it," Margie decided. I heard a few more placenta stories after that.

A few years ago I was looking after several sick parrots for a breeder and one was bitten by a viper when I was beside the cage. The snake slithered off as the parrot quickly expired in my hands.

I brought it to the house and Wayan Manis and I agreed it should have a nice burial in the garden with plenty of flowers. I went off to answer the phone, got distracted and came back a couple of hours later to find that the parrot had disappeared. Assuming it had been respectfully buried with appropriate ceremony, I opened the fridge door for a snack. Neatly wrapped in a plastic bag between the carrots and the yogurt was the parrot, its toes now tightly clenched in rigor mortis. "Kajang Kliwon," intoned Wayan Manis. Everyone knows you can't dig in the garden on Kajang Kliwon; the parrot was on ice until tomorrow. Susan reports that when her oldest koi committed suicide by jumping out of the pond late one afternoon she tenderly wrapped it up and put it in the fridge overnight so it could have a proper burial when the gardener arrived.

I am fortunate in knowing a trio of delightfully mad herps (reptile fanciers) in Ubud who are all perfectly capable of pulling a live snake out of their backpacks to be admired at any given moment. Don tells me that many reptile keepers today hibernate their turtles, tortoises, snakes and lizards in the fridge; there are even refrigerators specifically built for this purpose. In temperate species, a cooling-off period is necessary to allow males to develop viable sperm and females to be keyed into seasonal reproductive times (they chill out now so they can steam up later). Some very specialized keepers also keep cold-loving amphibians in fridges. Next time you visit your local herp, crack open that fridge door and see what's neatly lined up on the shelves. Slumbering serpents? Tranquil toads?

Don disclosed that dedicated breeders and collectors of birds and reptiles commonly keep very rare creatures that have died in their freezers in the hope that they can be useful to science. He showed me a few rare tortoises in zip lock bags next to the ice cream. I was able to tell him I'd heard of weirder things than that.

Ron, Bali's Snake Patrol guy, keeps unusual snakes frozen for the same reason, eventually preserving them with formalin for posterity. He also keeps a stock of frozen snakes for thawing out in case he's lucky enough to acquire a snake-eating snake such as a krait or king cobra. "I always have bags of frozen rats and mice in the freezer as well," he confides. "Not many, though -- they take up a lot of room which makes my wife cross. It's rather a small freezer."

Ron also told me that he occasionally keeps various insects and other invertebrates such as spiders in the fridge. "You just put them in there long enough to cool them down so they can be photographed without them running, jumping or flying away," he explained. "This is a well-known trick of wildlife photographers, especially for butterflies, but one has to be extra careful not to leave the beasties in the fridge too long, as prolonged exposure to cold will take them to the point of no return."

I grew up in bear territory in Canada. The municipal rubbish collectors came just once a week. No sensible householder would leave meat bones and other kitchen waste in the big plastic bin in the carport or a hungry bear would come lurking around and tear it open. So the food scraps were kept in the freezer and only placed in the bin on the morning of collection. But as my mother grew older, she would often forget. Opening the freezer door we would find the space full of unlabelled bags which would all have to be opened to ascertain whether they contained old bones or strawberries.

Elizabeth used to euthanize cane toads in her Australian freezer as being the most humane way to kill these deadly pests. Mary Jane put a valuable old book in the freezer to kill the bugs that were eating the paper. I routinely freeze heritage rice for a couple of days to kill insect eggs, but this does not seem as noteworthy to my friends as the bags of blood.

So be forewarned when you open someone else's freezer. There may be something very interesting indeed behind the frozen peas…

In Darkest Domestica

I don't do much housework in Bali. I am not naturally inclined to it and besides, Wayan Manis doesn't let me. When I make my own bed she shakes her head and does it again, with neater corners. She refuses to show me how to use the new washing machine. And she's been known to hide the broom on me, which is inconvenient when she disappears for days to attend ceremonies.

Things are very different when I go to Canada to visit my nonagenarian parents. My father is in a care facility now and my mother still lives in their apartment with her ancient cat. During my stays I wash dishes, do laundry, stock the freezer with nutritious meals, drive between the two residences, clean the cat box, make beds and pick up all the bits and pieces that end up on the floor because Mama lives in a stronger field of gravity than most of us mortals. Oh, and second-guessing her ailments. One night she was up with a dodgy tummy. I anxiously reviewed the previous night's dinner menu, but close questioning revealed that she had eaten half a box of chocolates after I'd gone to bed.

On my most recent visit, my sister Beth and I decided to take this pair of naughty elders on a trip to her home on the east coast of

Vancouver Island. The undertaking was planned with the attention to detail usually reserved for military campaigns. It was in fact reminiscent of preparing for a road trip with a couple of large, wilful toddlers. Six bags of luggage were packed for a two-night trip. Diapers (don't flinch, we are all going there), favourite blankets, hot water bottles, snacks, drinks, warm clothes, walking sticks, medication and a large bottle of gin were loaded into Beth's roomy van. We strapped in Mama first then went to spring Papa from what he calls his Velvet Prison. He parked his walker in a corner and chugged through the parking lot as fast as his white cane would allow. (He is always trying to get us to tell him the code to the locked gate so he can go for unsupervised walks.) We were off.

It was a long day of driving and sitting on the ferry, and we reached the house rather weary in late afternoon. This is temperate rainforest country; the trees were dense, the sky overcast and the wind cold. But inside the fire was lit and Beth's husband Tim was cooking a fragrant chicken stew. Mama and Papa were tucked into armchairs by the crackling fire with a large dog and cat in attendance. Cocktails were poured. It was assumed that the elders would catch a nap as they usually did throughout the day. But neither of them snoozed for a single moment during the whole weekend. I think we were all realizing that this might be the last family outing of them all.

Papa was particularly pleased to be out of his safe, comfortable but rather dull care facility. He is legally blind, incontinent, falls down a lot and is occasionally delightfully delusional but on the whole he's very much on the ball. A modest man, he copes well with his loss of privacy now that his personal needs are being met by caregivers. "This morning I had a shower with a woman whose name I didn't even know," he confided during dinner.

Tim roasted a turkey for lunch the next day and old family friends come to share it. Both parents ate like loggers, washing down the meal with plenty of wine. Mama demanded to be taken shopping. Papa was driven to nearby Saratoga beach, where he sat on a log and remembered bringing us to this very patch of sand for a summer holiday over five decades earlier. Later they consumed a large dinner, followed by dessert. They are both so tiny, where do they put it all?

At night, Beth and I took turns to sleep in the same room with Papa, as he tends to wander. I'm an enthusiastic sleeper, so I forced myself to stay awake all night because he was up and about every hour or two, disoriented in this strange environment. At one point I dozed off and woke just in time to intervene as he was preparing to irrigate a corner of the laundry room, having lost his bearings on the way to the loo. A sense of humour is absolutely essential in the aging process.

And it's earnestly to be hoped that a sense of humour will survive and thrive as I forge my own path to antiquity. With such robust genes, I might well have another three decades ahead of me. The developed world is struggling to care for its aging population but here in Indonesia the extended family is still the only fall-back. With so many foreigners choosing to retire here, we need to do some realistic forward planning around our own aging.

The medical care in Bali continues to improve, and hip and knee replacements, stents and cataracts can all be dealt with to international standards in Denpasar. But anything to do with gerontology and dementia is still pretty much off the radar.

Since 2002, divisions of geriatric medicine have been established in the departments of internal medicine in all Indonesia's government universities. But it's a rare doctor, either here or in the west, who chooses to specialise in it. Old people's problems are just not sexy. So this rapidly growing demographic (in 35 years, over a fifth of the world's population will be over 60) is not getting much attention.

I didn't pay much attention myself, until I had to start dealing with my parents' aging issues. Then a couple of years ago my own friends started to fall and break their hips and have the aforementioned cataract surgeries, stents and other age-related procedures we thought were for old people. It was astonishing to find that the medical community here considered us to BE old people. That can't be right. We're not ready.

I was also astonished and indignant to learn that my medical insurance company, to which I have been writing increasingly generous checks for 25 years, plans to ditch me when I turn 72. After some research I found out that most medical insurance plans have upper age limits, and few will accept new clients after the age of 65. In the face of a rapidly aging but largely healthy and active population, this has to change.

So here we sit, still feeling pretty frisky, with all these interesting issues ahead of us. We can eat well, exercise, and otherwise take good care of ourselves but the clock is ticking. Keep that sense of humour sharpened and get those domestic ducks in a row. It could be a long ride.

Every Second Wednesday

When I moved to Ubud sixteen years ago, I contacted the Editor of the Bali Advertiser with the suggestion that I write a column. I hardly knew anyone and it seemed like a good way to meet interesting people and find out what was going on.

I had no idea what I was getting into. I'd been a writer for many years and I knew what a deadline was, but these were remorseless. Every second Wednesday I had to pony up with 1,200 words that were interesting, relevant and true whether I felt like it or not. Sometimes I did not feel like it. Very often I sat down under the ticking clock with no idea at all what I was going to write about.

And so began a journey and a journal. I became a window to Bali and my life here for myself and BA readers. It wasn't supposed to be like this. Greenspeak was meant to be a column on the environment. But those endless deadlines soon pushed me out of that box, and I began to expand my mandate to include my own environment – my garden, my dogs, my staff, my street. I found myself holding the space for many small encounters and experiences and distilling them into 1,200 words of prose every second Wednesday. My editor, bless him, gave me a very long rope. (The only time he censored anything I've written was to remove a red-hot and possibly actionable paragraph about a manufacturer of baby formula.)

The column led me outside to meet people who are creating positive change on this island, onto construction sites, into rice fields and Balinese compounds. It led me into my garden to observe the plants and creatures there. And it led me inside myself, to examine how I was so touched by Bali's profound and quirky magic.

People tend to believe what they read in a newspaper and be influenced by it. So I had to train myself to be a witness, not a judge. Even if a situation had me raging, I had to try and present it from a place of calm balance because you will read it. I have to walk the talk, because of you. You keep me honest.

People my age who settle in this part of Bali often come from an academic or business life. They've taken a great leap of faith, leaving a world of reliable medical care, live theatre and affordable wine to live by a rice field. It's remarkable what happens to them, over time. The right side of the brain wakes up and starts to dance in Ubud, this little town that is a crucible of creativity. Tax lawyers and computer wizards take up painting, educators start designing hats. I used to write corporate brochures and advertising copy. Now my keyboard clicks to tales of spirits from the undercliff and dragons in the bath.

I'm always pleased and humbled when people tell me they enjoy reading my column. It's an odd feeling, actually, to write a story and send it out to the world for strangers to read and interpret through their own lens of experience. Sometimes those strangers write to me, and some of them become friends. A couple of times an enraged reader has sent in a rant – my writing was too positive, too happy. Was I blind? Didn't I see the piles of garbage and the mangy dogs and the corruption? Well yes, I do. But long ago I learned that people are just about as happy as they decide to be, and I've decided to be happy.

For years people have been saying, "You should make a book of these stories." But I'd written a book before, and dealt with agents, editors and publishers. I remembered the negotiations and compromises;

it hadn't been happy experience. Then one day photographer Ian Lloyd, himself a writer of books, said, "Just do it yourself. Make the book." And he told me how.

Someone once said, "Community begins exactly and precisely where you are sitting right now." In 2009 I set out to publish my first book, 'Bali Daze'. When I launched the project, I discovered that my community included all the people I needed to birth a book. Jenny helped select the stories. Diana edited the manuscript and Kathy proofed it. Susan executed a delightful water colour for the cover of the first edition.

When it was dry we took it to Sue's internet shop to scan and send to Singapore where Jenny's company would lay out the cover design. Jeremy advised on a local graphic designer and which type of paper to use. Trisna told me how to get an ISBN number, and Alex translated the letter. Bayu laid out the manuscript with saintly patience as I sat beside him, then reformatted the whole thing again when I got the dimensions wrong. Jean and William and Vern advised on marketing. Graeme designed the website. Janet placed the first order for 30 books. And everyone else said, "Well, it's about time." 'Bali Daze' has gone into four print runs since 2009.

This book you are holding went together in a few weeks, now that I know how to do it. Assembling the stories and looking back, I see what a magical journey my life in Bali has been. 'Aging in Place' is defined as "the ability to live in one's own home and community safely, independently and comfortably, regardless of age, income, or ability level." My friends and I are doing just that, getting older on our own terms and within modest resource bases. This book is about an unpretentious life in a Bali that many visitors and residents never see. A tourist in Kuta or a villa-dweller from the Bukit would think I was on another planet, not just up the road. Of course, we're all on our own planets, really. But here in Bali, nobody minds.

Animal Days

Life is never dull in my little garden behind the temple. When I wrote this piece the cast included myself, three dogs, two parrots, some chickens and a few turtles.

A certain amount of alertness is necessary to ensure that I'm first on the scene if the parrot hits the floor within range of a much-too-interested canine. And the dogs themselves had issues. The relationship between Daisy and Kalypso had always been uneasy and even confrontational; nocturnal dogfights under my bed were not unknown. A visit from Bali's own Dog Whisperer changed my wild pack into attentive and obedient canines in a single day by establishing me as Mega Alpha Plus Top Dog. Even now all I have to do is click my tongue, point a finger and dog bottoms hit the tile. Now I only have to worry about the dogs killing birds and reptiles instead of each other.

My rescued street dog Hamish can leap the two metre high garden wall like a deer. Although I constantly asked him to stay within the confines of the yard for his own safety, there was a much more exciting world outside the walls. He liked to visit the neighbours, check out the smells on our street and leave his mark a little higher on our front gate post than the dogs from the warung. But most of all he liked to visit the temple.

We live close to the Tebesaya Pura Dalem Puri with (to a dog) its intriguing smells and the possibility of interesting snacks. During big ceremonies several hapless pigs are sacrificed in the temple kitchen near the river. Hamish would disappear for lengthy periods and return with a sated expression and a distended tummy. During these excursions he was been known to purloin whole pig skulls and somehow drag them home over the wall.

The first time this happened, I was aghast to find the front path strewn with what looked like human teeth. I sometimes find these grisly molars on the verandah; once, expecting company, I kicked them furtively into the fishpond. Now that the turtles have eaten all the pond plants they are fully visible on the bottom. This does not help my reputation. I have to remember to warn houseguests about this, and also not to be alarmed if they see the dogs gnawing on what uncannily resembles fragments of a human jaw.

Lately Ibu, the female dog attached to the warung at the corner, has been in heat. The nights echo with the sound of madly barking dogs and ferocious dog fights, to which my own pack responds with enthusiastic howls from the confines of my bedroom. Every unaltered male dog on the street, and there are many, bears the scars of recent contests for Ibu's affections. The other morning I left my house to find Ibu in the very act, firmly attached to a scabby mongrel directly in front of the elementary school gate. Another dog was trying to make it a threesome and yet another was politely waiting his turn. A huddle of small boys watched disapprovingly from the gate, flicking the devoted pair with water from time to time. "Goodness," said a visiting friend. "You don't see much of this in England."

Then there are the birds. Rama the rescued parrot prefers to be known as Big Bird. "Hi, Big Bird, I love you!" he frequently affirms. Since I don't allow mirrors in his cage, he has no way of knowing that he is in fact a bald and unlovely bird; he thinks he's an eagle. "Perfect Bird," I sometimes hear him crooning to himself.

Big Bird has a new portable perch, cobbled together from pruned garden branches. It sits in the middle of the dining table on a strategically placed newspaper, and he likes to sit here and observe me tapping on the computer. The perch is hung about with toys and beads that last about a day under his busy beak. Big Bird is quickly bored when his playthings have been destroyed, and casts about for further entertainment. He likes papers and pens but has a special weakness for keyboards of all kinds.

On the afternoon I proudly brought my new laptop computer home and started to work on the outside table, Big Bird strolled over and pecked one of keys off completely. No one has ever been able to repair it. Once I went inside for a few minutes and came back to find him sitting on his perch with my hand phone, an old Nokia at that time, in his claw. He had removed the keypad cover and flung it aside, and all the phone lights were flashing. When I snatched it back, I saw that he had punched a three-line message onto the screen. (It looked like nonsense to me, but what do I know?) Luckily I was able to reassemble the phone and it still worked, but since then he constantly tries to grab it from my hand. Presumably he is waiting for a call.

Chiko, another rescue parrot, often sat on my shoulder while I wrote, grooming my hair and trying to remove my earring. This bird was absolutely gorgeous but had the personality of a potato. He spent hours in the same position staring at a fixed point in space, perhaps in meditation. When I offered him a peanut, it could take him a minute or two to process the information and actually accept it. But, like so many of us, he was motivated by sugar.

I was sipping tea one day when Chiko, perched on my shoulder, indicated interest. This was unusual, so I tilted the mug in his direction. He dove in for a sip and since then has insisted on sharing my tea every afternoon. Visitors consider this unhygienic, so I gave him his own cup. Although Chiko never did demonstrate much in the way of intellectual aptitude, he figured out that cups of tea often arrive on a tray along with milk and sugar. When the tea tray was placed on the table he would climb down from the perch, march resolutely across the table and dip his fluorescent orange beak into the silver sugar bowl. He was also very fond of arak.

On a recent visit to Canada I found my parent's apartment almost uncannily quiet; the only animal was an elderly cat. It made me realize how extraordinary my ordinary days with my animals have become, and how rich.

In Celebration of the Simple Life

I recently returned from almost a month in Canada, most of it spent in a shoebox of an apartment 25 floors above the earth. It's such a relief to have my feet on the ground again and take stock of my small, simple and very contented Ubud life.

Living in Vancouver is so complicated on many levels. There's weather, so people need lots of different clothes for every season. Coats, jackets, sweaters, office clothes, party clothes, sports clothes, doing-the-laundry clothes. And the footwear... rain boots, dress boots, running shoes, office shoes, sandals. It all takes up a great deal of space and is costly. I spend most of my day in Ubud in a sarong, barefoot.

We have weather here too, of course. But the beauty of living in the tropics is that a change of weather usually means taking clothes off instead of putting more on, or closing a window if you've got one. If it's raining hard while I'm out, I take off my shoes so they won't get spoiled. Watching me do this once, a friend told me how she stripped down to her stylish black bra and knickers during a heavy rain in Ubud, stashing her outer clothes in her back pack for the wet drive home on her motorbike. Just common sense, really.

Western kitchens are astonishingly complicated. There are vast numbers of cupboards full of dishes, glasses, pots, tools, electrical gadgets and exotic foods from the four corners of the world. It's amazing how much stuff people have. Discreet questioning reveals that no, my friends don't actually have the time or calorie allowances to make Belgian waffles, smoked lamb sausages or pressed duck, but they hang onto the equipment just in case. One such kitchen boasted several cupboards full of appliances but the owner confessed that she really only used the coffee press and the martini shaker, which don't even require electricity.

Inspired by the sight of so much largesse, I went crazy and upgraded my vegetable steamer to a state-of-the-art silicone one and bought an unnecessary but entertaining egg slicer. At a second hand shop I found some pretty mugs to replace the ones that constantly succumb to the powerful field of gravity that surrounds my housekeeper Wayan Manis. That's about it. I become overwhelmed in western stores now. There's too much stuff in there and I often leave without buying anything.

During my visit I was reminded that keeping a dog in Canada is a serious commitment of time and money. My niece recently bought a long-haired purebred canine for a thousand dollars. It requires much daily brushing, costly food and medical insurance to cover the spectacularly expensive bills it generates for genetic and gastric disorders. It spends most of its day in a cage in the apartment while its mistress is at work. She spends hours a day before and after work walking the dog and it goes to doggy day care twice a week to learn social skills. No dog is ever seen outside without its human; I believe this is now illegal in Canada.

I explained all this to Hamish. He rested his long muzzle on my knee, his brown eyes deeply puzzled. Hamish declines to be brushed or confined and the one time I tried to take him for a walk on a leash he bucked, shimmied and ultimately slipped his collar before disappearing into the nearest compound. He much prefers to take himself for walks and his social skills are just fine, thank you.

Then there's the deceptively simple act of going out for a coffee. In Canada I needed to study the complex menus in the coffee shops and be ready to recite my order when my turn came in the queue. Size of cup, provenance of the beans, darkness of the roast, how it should be brewed, depth of froth, genesis of the milk (cow, soy, almond) and several other critical elements. At the end of the day it didn't hold a candle to the screamingly fresh Arabica beans that are delivered to my door every week in Ubud, ground while the kettle of spring water is boiling, brewed simply in a French press and sipped while watching blossoms drift from the frangipani trees.

There's the whole culture of bottled drinking water. Clever marketing and branding have elevated the cost of bottled water in Canada to well above that of petrol. No one would dream of drinking water from the tap. Nor would we in Ubud, but I haven't bought water for years. Everyone on my street draws their water from a spring that's distributed through a tap in the temple grounds. In early mornings and late afternoons it's reminiscent of a village well as the Balinese gather to gossip and patiently wait to fill their water receptacles. That's where Wayan Manis picks up the latest gossip as she waits her turn, Hamish sitting patiently beside her. I filter the water, which is delicious, but no one else on the street does. It's from a temple spring, after all. What could go wrong?

In Vancouver I plotted my course to the passport office on public transport, changing from bus to ferry to train. It was either that or navigate the city in my mother's car, and the many traffic rules and concealed cameras made me anxious after 25 years of Asian street anarchy. In Ubud I can walk almost everywhere. I live a few minutes stroll from the centre of town, right at the edge of the Financial District (yes, we have one). Or I hitch a lift on the back of Wayan Manis' motorbike. The old car is only used for adventures out of town and during the rainy season.

Simplicity. The house runs on under 1000 watts of electricity except when we use the iron or washing machine. Besides olive oil, butter and a few condiments I seldom eat anything imported. For years I've had a little ritual -- the first food I put in my mouth every day is from my garden. Sometimes it's papaya and eggs. Sometimes it's tomatoes or a few mulberries or an avocado. When it's been raining for months, it might be just greens. But it's very personal, that first taste. It nourishes the soul.

Before I moved from Singapore to Ubud it took me six months to clear the stuff out of my old house. And, Singapore being so affluent, no one wanted most of it so a lot of perfectly good things went to the dump. That was a lesson. Once here, I built a small house with no storage so I wouldn't be tempted to slip back into the consumer mentality.

Life is as simple or as complicated as we decide to make it. For an entertaining yet sobering overview on consumerism, go to www.storyofstuff.org The 20 minutes it takes to watch could change your buying habits forever. If we live simply and don't buy much stuff or processed food, then we don't support the giant corporations who depend on endless consumerism in order to thrive. We can support farmers markets for our produce and have favourite clothes copied by local tailors. In our own small way, we can support local small businesses and producers in Bali instead of giant multinationals. It's simple, really.

It Wasn't Always Like This

Recently when I was stuck in an increasingly ubiquitous traffic jam in Ubud I noticed a bumper sticker on the car in front of me that read, 'Bali is Not New York'. Now, I would have thought this was already pretty clear. Built up as it now is, still no one is likely to mistake Jalan Ubud Raya for Fifth Avenue. Then I realized that people who come here for the first time probably think Bali's always been like this, with hot croissants delivered to your door, Italian bathroom fixtures, air-conditioned restaurants and traffic jams. (This is the view from Ubud, of course. I never venture south of Mas.)

Fifteen years ago Ubud residents rejoiced to find a loaf of decent bread or real cheese. When we were building our houses we could choose from shiny white, blue or dark red floor tiles. Paint was in primary colours. Choices were few. Now that every warung has WiFi and you can order a cappuccino at every corner, people seem to think it's always been like this. Folk who move here now often expect everything to work perfectly and to be on time, just like the 'real world'. So it's quite interesting to observe how Bali, under this thin veneer of modernity, gently reminds the newcomers that this particular world is real in a different way.

It wasn't always like this and it still isn't, sometimes. When those times come, it's easy to separate the ones who will put down roots from those who are operating under the delusion that Bali is a suburb of Sydney.

When my friend Jenny contracted the house next door, she knew what she was getting into. She's been visiting me here since 2000 and shared all kinds of dramas. Of course, the renovations weren't quite complete when she finally moved in and brought her family from England for a holiday. Within two weeks Bali presented her with a typical welcome wagon of events. First was the freak weather pattern that delivered unseasonal rain in ropes and torrents, night and day, until the garden was a swamp. The long pathway from the road hadn't been landscaped yet (because all the labourers were in Java for Idul Fitri) so every visitor brought along a kilo of mud on his shoes. The nice white cement floor, polished to an obsessive sheen, was constantly dirty. Jenny dealt with this by taking the family north to the beach.

Then there was the electricity blackout that plunged the whole island into dense darkness. She lit a few candles and the family played cards. A week or so later she woke early to enjoy a solitary cup of tea on the patio. Dreamily lounging on her new bench sipping a herbal brew, it took her a few moments to register that the coconut trunk pillars supporting the house were bending in unison and the roof was undulating. In fact, it was a respectable earthquake. A minute later I got a text message, "Goodness, that was a big one!"

Jenny and her family quickly adapted to 'The Hole' and the fact that social events and dining decisions were made according to what side of The Hole you live on because the long detour by Monkey Forest Road could mean 45 minutes in traffic. (For newcomers, The Hole was a giant sinkhole that appeared in front of Ubud Market one night and remained unmended for about six months, effectively cutting the town in half.) She didn't blink when her gardener captured and removed a green pit viper from near her outdoor kitchen. In short, an ideal candidate for life in Ubud. If you're not flexible, cheerful and curious the issues associated with living here could get you down.

Then there are the whiners, complaining constantly about the garbage, the traffic and the state of the infrastructure. Yes, the lights go out, the water stops running and things are constantly breaking down. I frequently hear, "Why don't They make the tourist buses park outside of town? Why don't They protect Ubud's character? Can't They do something about the garbage /the sidewalks/the dogs?"

Good people, there is no They.

This comes as a stunning revelation to those who grew up in ordered, well-managed communities where They are firmly in control. They make laws and ensure compliance. You can call Them up and complain about things, and They will often respond. But this is a little farming community that grew organically into an arts-focused tourist town and is now morphing into – heaven help us – an 'alternative destination'. The members of whatever local government exists have no experience in town planning. Life used to be very simple here, not so long ago. Growing numbers of tourists and residents bring money, yes. But they also stretch the inadequate infrastructure past its tolerance, and this is not a culture that plans ahead.

There's uncontrolled development in Bali because we outsiders choose to visit and live here, so it seems fair that we seek ways to be part of the solution. There are scores of projects going on, managed by Rotary Clubs, individuals and NGOs. Plenty of concerned Balinese would welcome some technical assistance in solving local problems. You don't have to travel very far off the main roads to find poverty, ignorance and treatable medical conditions. There's plenty of community work to be done, and becoming engaged in it softens some of the hard edges our coming here has caused.

Bali is not New York. It's a small, fragile island with a unique cultural heritage, sinking under the weight of millions of foreigners and their expectations. The Balinese didn't know we would come in such numbers. They didn't know we would build houses and stay. They don't know quite what to make of us and our 'real world' expectations, iced cappuccinos and swimming pools. It wasn't always like this.

There's Something About Hamish

Hamish arrived early in 2005, a street dog with a hideous case of mange. Rescued by BAWA and treated at BARC, he was a terrible mess when I saw him for the first time. The parasites had eaten through the skin of his back deep into the flesh, from ears to tail. I crouched beside him at the shelter; looking into his eyes I saw a great soul in that tortured body. "Would you like to come home with me?" I asked. He closed his expressive brown eyes, laid his head on my foot and gave a deep sigh.

We wrapped him in a towel and he was placed on my lap for the brief journey home. He'd probably never been in a lap before, but he was very good about it. The journey itself was less successful; he was spectacularly carsick.

I placed him on the grass just inside the gate and told him he was welcome to join us when he felt like it. The other two dogs came and sniffed him once or twice but otherwise he was left to explore his new territory. It took him all day to work himself from the front gate to the patio.

My quiet compound and regular meals were a big shift from the chaos and uncertainty of the street. Hamish lived on the outskirts of our family for the first month while he got to know us and found his balance. He slept outside because, frankly, he smelled awful.

I was unsure if this street dog would know how to behave in the house but he was a perfect gentleman from the beginning. (All Bali dogs seem to be housebroken from birth.) He was also patient and well-mannered, allowing me to paint his wounds with potions of aloe vera and turmeric juice. The first few months were challenging for us both. He hated the mange injections and when he started to scream every time he saw a needle, we switched him to the oral dose. His skin was so inflamed that some nights he literally glowed in the dark. Every time he grew in some hair, it would fall out and there were clouds of it everywhere.

A year later when his skin was beginning to clear and his hair to grow he showed symptoms of genital sarcoma, a sexually transmitted canine cancer. We started chemotherapy, which meant three long journeys to Denpasar for the very carsick dog on my lap; even a large bath towel was inadequate protection. Wayan Manis would wait for our return at the gate and hose us both down as soon as we arrived.

Hamish bounced back from the cancer, a year of Ivermectin for the parasites and being relieved of his testicles on the dining table. When his hair grew in he became recognizable as a handsome specimen, a mix of Bali Heritage dog with Kintamani blood who proceeded to win hearts at the speed of light.

There's something about Hamish. Even people who don't particularly like dogs want to take him home. One friend said she could picture him sitting on the plane seat next to hers at 35,000 feet politely eating off his tray. He's a very handsome chap and he knows it. His melting gaze and the gentle tap of his paw on your knee sucks you in like a vortex, and before you know it you're slavishly rubbing his tummy and telling him how much you love him.

Plainly, having a home had its advantages. But he'd spent his early years on the street and he hated being confined. Even my big, shady garden wasn't enough territory and he found his way under, over and through walls more than two metres high to join his insalubrious friends in the temple parking lot and roll in rotting offerings.

Nocturnal ramblings took him next door where he'd jump up to sleep on my friend's daybed, muddy feet and all. He would be sighted as far away as Jalan Hanoman. I briefly tried to leash him and take him for walks but he quickly learned to slip the harness. At least I was really walking. The Balinese notion of taking the dog for a walk is to put it on a leash, stroll to the corner and hang out with their friends for a smoke while the dog sits beside them, then stroll home.

Hamish is a popular visitor at Pura Dalem Puri, the temple next to my house. Wayan Manis reports that when a pig is slaughtered for a ceremony, Hamish is right there with the men of the banjar, sitting politely beside them soliciting scraps and observing them as they make the ritual lawar.

He has a gift for making every person he's with believe that he worships him or her alone and can't live without them. Then he goes next door and puts on the same act for someone else. One year when I had two women neighbours in adjacent houses he demonstrated his skill in harem management. The moment I'd go out he would start on his rounds. First he'd visit Heather and convince her that she was the most important person in his life, showering her with adoring glances and whimpers while she hand-fed him treats. She'd text triumphantly to Jen and I, "Hamish is here with me, he loves me the best." Ten minutes later we'd hear from Jen. "He's with me now, his eyes are so eloquent, clearly he loves me best." But I didn't mind; he slept in my room at night, although sometimes I had to text around and get his current lady friend to send him home at bedtime.

Hamish is absolutely never allowed on the furniture. I learned that my house sitter Esther used to let him sleep with her in my bed when I was away. Now this bed is a Chinese antique, beautifully carved and gilded, but only 125 cm wide. It's perfectly comfortable for one small woman but Esther is tall and Hamish is a big boy. When I enquired how they adjusted themselves to the limited real estate she said, "Oh, he slept on top of me with his head on my shoulder! It was so romantic." Later Di, another tall house sitter, confessed that she too had permitted this infraction at considerable discomfort to herself. It's no wonder he has entitlement issues.

Hamish is part Kintamani, Bali's only official breed. Genetic studies show that the Kintamani dog is native to Bali and distinct from the more common Bali Heritage Dog. One hypothesis for the genesis of the Kintamani is that sometime between the 12th and 16th centuries a Chinese trader landed in Singaraja in Northern Bali, bringing with him a Chow Chow dog which bred with the local Balinese feral dogs. This is quite likely, since the Chinese are known to have been travelling to Bali for at least 2,000 years.

My friend Charlotte, who has been keeping Kintamani dogs here for 15 years, says a purebred Kintamani is not for everyone. "You have to understand the individual personality and the character of the dog," she told me. "They can be very sensitive, even to a raised voice, and have their own agendas. It's a relationship, both sides have to work at it. The Kintamani needs to be the only dog in the family, he has to be the king of the castle."

When Charlotte's original Kintamani died a couple of years ago, she sent a trusted Balinese friend to a village he knows where pure bred Kintamanis are still raised. She says they breed in the rainy season, and that the bitches dig deep holes in which to birth their puppies. Different families breed white, black or white and brown dogs. Now that the Kintamani is a recognized breed more people are breeding them just for the money, which will have an impact on the bloodlines.

Hamish is about 12 years old now, and can no longer heave his corpulent self over the garden walls. He asks to be let out twice a day to do his rounds but quickly comes home. His wandering days are over. He is not pure Kintamani; he lacks the double coat and the proud personality. But there's something about Hamish, something distinctive and engaging. And he definitely has his own agenda.

A Table's Tale

When I moved to Ubud in 2000 I rented a small house on Jalan Andong. It was not a very nice house but there wasn't much on the rental market at that time. The previous renter had left me a thin mattress on the floor, a plastic stool and a small fridge containing three jars of mayonnaise (he was Dutch). There was also a resident ghost that stole my tools and plenty of big sawah spiders which I had not yet learned to love.

It would be weeks before my small shipment of furniture would arrive from Singapore and meanwhile the cottage was essentially bare. It was the rainy season. The roof leaked. Looking around my cheerless abode I decided that I needed at least a table where I could sit and contemplate my nasi bungkus.

I found a driver, explained my mission and we slowly cruised the then-sleepy main drag of Mas where the furniture warehouses were. I have a low shopping threshold; after the third stop I will buy just about anything in order to be allowed to go home. I saw some not very nice tables for which unreasonable sums were requested and resigned myself to more picnics on the floor. After the third shop I'd had enough, but the driver suggested just one more place.

And bingo, there it was, the just-right table. A metre wide and two metres long, it was big enough to have ongoing projects at one end and lunch at the other. It was made of sustainable woods -- recycled teak and coconut. It would seat eight for dinner, my favourite number of guests. And the price was just what I'd had in mind. The table was delivered the next day. I sat on the plastic stool and ate my lunch and placed a jar of leaves and flowers in the centre. Suddenly the empty house felt more like a home.

If tables could talk, this one would have tales to tell.

Soon I took custody of a rescued puppy named Karma, my very first dog. Shortly afterward I met a visiting English vet who was bringing supplies to Janice Girardi for her work with street dogs which would evolve into the Bali Animal Welfare Association (BAWA). He decided that Karma was old enough for The Snip and we located the only practicing small animal vet in Ubud at that time. It turned out that this vet had never actually operated on a real dog before although he had read about it in a book. The Englishman offered to help him and the two men disappeared into a back room with the puppy. (A minute later the visiting vet left briefly and returned with a newly purchased light bulb. He later reported that the clinic 'operating room' was illuminated by a dusty 5 watt bulb and he had hardly been able to see the dog, much less the equipment.)

Karma recovered on a plump cushion under the table. But by the time the stitches were ready to come out, the visiting vet had left. I'd once worked for a surgeon and had taken out plenty of stitches in my time, but could hardly hold down a lively dog alone while removing small stitches from a tender part of his anatomy. Then I thought to invite over a couple of people I'd recently met for a drink. After a stiff gin and tonic I broached the subject and both gentlemen, to their credit, enthusiastically rolled up their sleeves. I sat cross-legged on the table with Karma on my lap, Graeme immobilized his feet and Guy delicately snipped away the stitches like the surgeon he wasn't. We celebrated with another drink. Karma got a biscuit.

Three months later when Karma died of distemper I laid my head down on the table and wept.

I missed having canine energy about the place. So I acquired Kipper, a bashful pit bull cross with major separation anxiety issues. After several weeks of chewed carpets, cushions, shoes and even potted plants I consulted my dog psychology books, which suggested that he needed a pet. Paolo was downsizing his pack and brought over Kalypso, an elegant Kintamani bitch. Kipper adored her and soon became less besotted with me. I was congratulating myself on my newly peaceful household when all the hormones kicked in at once. Very early one dark morning I was woken by canine vocalizations I'd never heard before. Sleepily opening the front door, I witnessed Kipper and Kalypso in energetic sexual union on the table. She did not appear to be enjoying it much, but intervention seemed inadvisable. More surgery soon followed this event.

A year later I built a house and of course the table came too. By this time I'd learned how central a table was in the grand scheme of households. If you had to strip life down to a few essentials the furniture would probably be a table, a chair and a bed. You can pretty much fake the rest.

The years rolled by. Friends celebrated and grieved around the table over a meal, a drink or a pot of tea. The dogs slumbered under it during storms. Maps were unrolled on it when journeys were being planned. When Wayan Manis sat at the table instead of starting her work for the day, it was a signal that a meeting was being called to discuss a loan, a wedding or a ceremony.

Dogs continued to arrive and depart. The table twice became an al fresco operating room when Topaz and later Hamish were deemed old enough for The Snip. It's much less traumatic for the dog to have this procedure in his own familiar territory and besides, Hamish became spectacularly carsick as soon as the engine started.

Then a friend visiting from Sydney decided that the time had come for her to acquire a long-considered tattoo. The Balinese artist arrived and together they pored over books of samples together and selected a design. Donna sat on the table with her back to the artist, who crouched on the bench behind her and spent the next hour drilling the small of her back with an electric needle as she alternately smoked furiously and swallowed arak while making faces.

When Patricia came out in a mysterious rash all over herself, a group of us placed a big towel on the table, laid Patricia naked on top of it like the main course and painted her all over with chilled aloe vera.

Rama the semi-feathered cockatoo likes to strut his stuff along the edge of the table. Now that I have chickens, they want a piece of the tabletop action as well. The older one likes to sneak into the house and roost at the foot of my bed. When this is prevented she hops up on the table instead, giving the term 'tabling a motion' a whole new meaning (you can't housetrain a chicken). Needless to add, the table is scrubbed a lot. Once a year or so Nyoman gets out the electric sander and takes off the top layer, giving us a new start. But the history of the table is deep in its grain now, with a patina of the energy left there by the friends and animals who have spent time on, under and around its warm wood.

Eat Pray Freeze – from Ubud to Umbria

I finally made it to Italy after several years of false starts. Looking forward to the refreshing temperatures of a European spring, I inadvertently invoked the coldest May in half a century. Bundled in layers of optimistically light clothing I wandered the cobbled streets of Orvieto, undertaking some serious research of a culinary nature. Between pasta encounters, I entertained myself by seeking parallels between this medieval town and my home in Ubud.

Both towns are cultural vortices, complete with their own powerful energies. They both attract mobs of tourists into their narrow streets, overpriced hotels and souvenir shops packed with merchandise of questionable quality and taste. Church bells in one, gamelans in the other. Medieval Europe had a strict caste system; the nobility was at the top, followed by the clergy, then soldiers, artisans, merchants and peasants -- exactly mirroring the caste system in Bali. But there were two similarities that I found particularly interesting — elements of their cuisines and the culture of devotion.

Both Italians and Balinese love pork, and whole roast pigs play an important role as festival food in both cultures. Sus scrofa, the Eurasian wild pig, was introduced in both places but has been hunted to extinction in Bali, which now relies on domesticated porkers. In the forests of Tuscany and Umbria, though, there are still all too many wild boar.

Until the 1950s wild boar populations in Italy were controlled by farmers who shot them for meat and to protect their crops. The abandonment of the countryside and marginal lands by farming families after the war allowed the boar to overtake new areas and breed unchecked. About the same time Italian hunters, who wanted to bolster the native stock, introduced Eastern European boar that are much larger and produce litters of up to 15 piglets.

The result has been a disaster for agriculture, with herds of boar destroying crops much the way deer do in some parts of North America. Only stone walls or electric fences will keep them out. One winemaker said his vineyard looked like it had been picked with a mechanical harvester after the boars paid a visit. I talked to a Tuscan farmer who said he no longer plants sunflowers, because the boars come through and destroy the whole crop overnight. A woman near Siena whose family has owned extensive gardens there for centuries said that the wild boar are now so numerous that hunters recently killed nine in a single night practically on her doorstep.

What happens to all these naughty piggies? It's not surprising that hunting clubs organise boar hunts during the fall, nor that boar is readily available in Italian supermarkets and appears often on restaurant menus in sauces and stews. The national favourite pork dish is porchetta, in which the boar is skinned, gutted, boned, rolled with herbs, seasoned and spit-roasted, very much like Bali's babi guling. A Panini Porchetta is roast wild boar sliced into a crusty roll, and very tasty too. One man told me that the wild boar were so delicious because they ate only the most tender of (stolen) vegetables and delicate forest plants.

Italians take their food very seriously. The Slow Food movement started here, and the concept of regional cuisine is strong. One restaurant boasted 'We prepare our dishes with ingredients from carefully selected peasants and shepherds in the Orvieto area.' They are very big on truffles in Umbria, and even put them in the gelato. The markets are full of gorgeous vegetables which, mysteriously, almost never appear on restaurant menus.

Bali and Italy also share an enjoyment of the coffee break, savouring frequent small cups or glasses of a strong, black brew throughout the day. The Italians take their espresso like a drug; they zoom into a coffee bar, tip at least one envelope of sugar into the tiny cup, stir it madly, knock it back in one gulp and zoom out again. Which brings up a curious point. Ubud's rents and wages are lower than those in Italy and our coffee comes from just up the hill, so why is a good cup of Arabica cheaper in Italy than it is here? Even in Rome you can get a coffee for a Euro.

I became a serious student of Italian coffee culture. I learned that a long black is called an americano, and that ordering cappuccino after noon is a serious cultural error. I practiced lounging around in outdoor cafes pretending to be from across the street, and got so good at it that several times Italians stopped to ask me for directions.

How can one not love a culture that offers hot pizza for breakfast, takes 90 minute lunch breaks, considers it reasonable to eat gelato at any time of day and sells perfectly drinkable wine for Rp 35,000 a bottle?

But enough about food, let's move on to prayer. Italian cathedrals and Balinese temples are the architectural manifestations of a devotion that was once universal in Italy and remains so in Bali. Etruscan and Roman stonework laid the literal foundations for innumerable cathedrals, churches, convents and monasteries in every Italian town and city. Although Catholicism is fading in Italy now, until about 50 years ago the culture was closely integrated with the Catholic church. For over a thousand years the Church dominated art, architecture, literature, festivals and many aspects of everyday life.

I've always loved the feeling of holy places of all kinds, even before I understood how centuries of devotion left an energetic signature in a building as physical as a coat of paint. I chose to stay in convents twice during the trip as an interesting alternative to hotels. Both convents were vast and ancient, with metre-thick walls.

Only three elderly nuns remained in each. I wandered endless mazes of chapels and chambers and staircases and hallways with vaulted ceilings and tiled floors. One convent had an ancient faded fresco in the breakfast room. In the other, I was the only person sleeping in the whole building. The silence within the thick walls was dense enough to cut with a knife, and so was the cold. Luckily there were plenty of quilts, and I curled up under several to consider the lives of the women who slept here hundreds of years ago.

Medieval nuns were often women of noble birth and considerable character. For women in those days, entering a convent was the only alternative to marriage (usually a business arrangement between the bridegroom and the bride's father in which she had no voice) and endless childbearing. Probably many were heartbroken lovers, women fleeing marriage, widows seeking security in old age or inconvenient girls placed there by their families. But the cloister was also the only place where medieval women with scholarly or artistic aspirations could study and work together.

The caste system was mirrored within convent walls. High-born nuns lived well and many became literate, a rarity at that time. The nuns from the lower social classes did the rough work. Nuns were the original nurses and teachers and founded the first hospitals and orphanages. But even for the well-born, winters in those huge, drafty stone rooms must have been grueling. Those women were tough.

Although Catholicism is little practiced now — those enormous, glorious cathedrals might see a dozen people for mass on Sundays — most Italian communities celebrate annual festivals dating from medieval times. Just as in Bali, streets and even whole towns close down for processions which often end in a feast.

Like the Balinese the people of Orvieto like to be outside, weather permitting. They're a sociable lot. When they meet for coffee, lunch or a glass of wine no one is checking their hand phones. They are fully engaged with each other. At the end of the day they gather in town squares, street corners, cafes and bars, talking excitedly as if they hadn't met for years and gesturing animatedly with both hands. It reminds me of my back alley in Ubud, where in late afternoon everyone, freshly bathed, gathers by their gates to gossip.

The weather finally cleared and the sun came out. Suddenly it was as hot as Ubud, and I began to miss my dogs. After a final lunch of fettuccini with wild boar sauce, I went to the airport. Italy is glorious but as Dorothy said, there's no place like home.

Gambols with Gastropods

In the rainy season, early mornings find me in the garden harvesting that most prolific of monsoon crops -- the garden snail. I'm a live-and-let-live creature most of the time, but my proximity to the jungle and the wet conditions bring forth Helix aspersa in legions. They chew holes in my tender heliconia leaves and devour infant seedlings overnight. So my garden is a Zero Tolerance Zone.

The garden snail seems to be one of those rare animals that has no natural enemies. I was told that ducks would eat them but when I offered some to my flock of Muscovies, they recoiled in horror. Rama the Bald Parrot, a sometime carnivore, flung a proffered snail from his cage in disgust. What was I to do with them all? Some mornings I was gathering a kilogram or more. I noticed that they liked to congregate in certain parts of the garden and left other areas severely alone. Likewise, they preferred certain plants. I've seen up to ten on a single papaya trunk, evidently holding an important meeting. They like to hang out on the underside of keladi leaves, they favour banana and ginger plants and also enjoy a foray into my precious mulberry trees. So on misty mornings I wander through the dripping leaves, plucking slimy gastropods from the greenery until my bucket runneth over.

When I go off to answer the phone, I return to find my prey escaping in all directions. According to the literature, the fastest are the speckled garden snails which can move several yards per hour compared with 23 inches per hour for most other land snails. The world record for speed seems to be held by a garden snail named Archie, who covered a 13 inch course in 2 minutes at the 1995 World Snail Racing Championships held in Longhan, England. No matter what speed they're moving at, snails leave a telltale track of gleaming silver behind them so they are easy to recapture. The thick slime they produce allows them to crawl along the edge of a razor without harm, should they wish to, and creates a suction that lets them travel upside down. Many land snails can lift ten times their own weight up a vertical surface. So they do have a few tricks.

At first I would reluctantly consign my daily catch to the liquid manure barrel (with a prayer for their rebirth as bees or butterflies) and truly they did not seem to suffer as they became part of the compost cycle, but the layer of snail shells became unwieldy. For a time I cast them up onto the thick wilderness of flowering vines on top of the parking garage until I noticed them sneaking back into the garden on damp nights. Since then I take them across the road to a patch of wilderness, but suspect they make a run for it back to my yard when I'm asleep.

For a few weeks before Christmas they held shameless orgies on the grass. Snails are hermaphrodites, which means that they have both male and female reproductive organs. What does a hermaphrodite look for in a mate, I wonder? Snails have very poor eyesight and cannot hear, so how do they find each other? Perhaps they just bump into one another while consuming my heritage vegetable seedlings and adjust their genders accordingly.

When they do locate a particularly attractive partner, a white (ahem) organ appears from both and pierces the slimy body of the other. Then they just lay around for hours on the grass like that in broad daylight; it's a scandal. I'm told that prior to reproduction, most land snails perform a ritual courtship before mating that can last anywhere from two to twelve hours but have not seen this. Prolific breeders, each snail may bury up to 100 fertilized eggs every month. No wonder there are so many of them. Quite a lot of these amorous couples went to Snail Heaven together in my compost bucket, but it didn't have an appreciable effect on the population. They keep on coming, remorselessly sliding up trees and under leaves and across the grass.

Wayan Manis took a big bag of them to a friend once to make satay, but there were no repeat orders. Presumably these are the escargot esteemed by gourmet diners; people have been eating freshwater snails and land snails since prehistoric times. Today they are still regarded as a delicacy in many countries. The market supply comes largely from snails that are raised in captivity on special farms in southern France, Italy, and Spain. I'm told there's a seasoning paste made of fermented garden snails in East Bali, and I'm happy to supply the raw material to any entrepreneurs desirous of setting themselves up in this business, absolutely free of charge.

Locally, some people do relish a dish of snails. Several hundred snails were found in a car in Sanur where they were escaping from the recent floods, and a Balinese acquaintance cooked them up for her family. Here's the recipe -- tip the snails into boiling water to kill them, then extract them from the shells and cut off the black tail. Simmer them with Balinese bumbu until tender and enjoy. You can have my share. The largest land snail ever found was 15 inches long and weighed 2 pounds, enough to feed an entire Balinese compound.

When not being harassed by murderous gardeners, a Helix garden snail will live for up to three years. Some of the big African species live for much longer and snails in captivity enjoy a lifespan of ten to fifteen years. This begs the question of why anyone would keep a snail, arguably low on the personality scale, as a pet. It does indeed take all kinds to make a world.

Without vision or hearing and presumably not much in the way of thinking equipment the Helix snail travels around aimlessly all night, often going around in complete circles. They rely mainly on their sense of touch to locate my tender seedlings, decaying leaves, fungi, cardboard and other food. A few types are carnivorous and even cannibalistic.

There are between 50,000 and 200,000 mollusk species alive in the world today. Many species have yet to be discovered and many recently discovered species are yet to be identified and named. Perhaps mine fall into that category, and will someday be known as Helix bewareofibukatoftebesaya.

The Turn of the Wheel

If you're an expat living far from elderly parents, you're always waiting for that phone call, the sibling's voice saying, "It's time to come back." And you park your life indefinitely and get on a plane. The wheel turns.

My father had a mild stroke a few years ago. He seemed to be getting over it, then relapsed, then rallied, then got an infection. I kept asking if I should return; not yet, said my sisters. Then came that call, "You'd better come now."

And so began ten weeks which in retrospect were the most precious of my life so far. A time when the margins between parent and child dissolve into a borderless pool of unconditional love, endless work, laughter and tears.

Papa was out of the hospital again when I arrived. At first he seemed as lucid and funny as ever, but I saw that he tired quickly. He leaned to one side and couldn't put his shoes on. He never knew what day it was (but that is a tricky question; neither do I, most of the time). He could tell me exactly how his infra-red headphones worked, but not what he'd had for breakfast. Sometimes he was not lucid at all. None of this bothered him as much as the fact that he had lost the ability to read. He was very bored and frustrated, and television didn't work for him any more either. His ambition was to be able to read the Economist again.

I borrowed a large-print book from the library, cut a hole in a piece of cardboard that revealed one line at a time, and we sat together every day until he could manage a full page. Then we used a ruler to focus on each line. By the end of three weeks he could read several pages of a book at a sitting and a paragraph of the Economist. We celebrated with a glass of sherry.

The days were exhausting. I made appointments with doctors and therapists, drove papa to meet them, kept notes, took him for walks, helped with his occupational therapy, monitored his meds, talked to the home care workers and did all the paperwork. My mother, also 89, was so overwhelmed by it all that she surrendered her jealously guarded kitchen to me. I shopped for and cooked all the meals, did laundry, took blood pressures… it was an endless blur of activity from morning until dark, when I collapsed in bed.

But we had a lot of fun. We decided that there had to be a lighter side to all of this, and we kept on looking until we found it. We found the humour when both my parents lost their hearing aids the same day, and when papa tried to fit both feet into the same pajama leg.

We kept looking for the lighter side of incontinence, but we never did find it.

My mother, always a bit impatient and difficult to please, was astonished to find herself married to a suddenly elderly and delusional man who listed slightly to starboard. She rebounded with humour and grace. After 62 years of sparring, they were sweetly tender with each other now.

Papa was anxious at night and would get up at three in the morning, dress himself and sit by the front door so he wouldn't be late for his morning appointment at physiotherapy. The sedative his doctor prescribed was evidently not working, so we increased the dose. The next morning I came into the bedroom to find my sister and mother tucked into one bed together sipping their coffee and my father prone in the other. "Perhaps we've gone too far," we mused. "My children are turning me into a junkie," muttered papa into his pillow. We went out for dinner that evening and he managed his meal as if the stroke had never happened.

It was time to sell the family home and move the parents into an independent living facility. Papa asked me if there was anything I wanted from the house before it was put on the market. All I wanted was his old Morse code key; he'd been a radio operator during the war but hadn't used his ham rig for years. Two days later he developed a serious blood infection and we rushed him to hospital. He lay there for a week, off with the fairies most of the time, with a catheter in his heart. But he recovered from that too and was home for his birthday.

I went out for groceries after we sprung him from the hospital and returned to find he'd already ditched his walker and gone into the basement alone. "And I have to go again," he told me determinedly when I reminded him of his promise not to use the stairs. I escorted him slowly down the steep steps and into his office, where he pointed a shaky hand at the Morse code key bolted to his desk. He had remembered. (I brought it home to Bali and mounted it on a piece of polished coconut wood.) But the infection had scrambled his eyes again and he could no longer read. This time, he wasn't even interested in the Economist. The wheel had turned beyond reading now.

By the time I left after that visit, they were both back in some kind of balance. There were home care workers, meals being delivered, all kinds of helpers and neighbours to keep an eye on them. I went back again two months later to move them into the assisted living facility, which is a bit like a cruise ship that doesn't go anywhere. We put the house on the market on a Tuesday morning, had three excellent offers by Friday and signed the papers that evening.

I went back to the house to pack for the last time. As I walked from one empty room to another I remembered the day we moved here, growing up, returning to stay as an adult and the recent months of nursing my parents. When I closed the door behind me for the last time, the wheel had turned full circle.

The Lighter Side of Urban Development

It started without warning one sunny day in November. Five men appeared early in the morning with the intention of breaking down the stone wall across the narrow lane from my gate. The wall held back a couple of meters of overgrown bank that separated the lane from a temple. 'Bongkar' is the delightful Indonesian word that means 'knock it down' and the blameless wall was soon being violently dismantled into its component parts by a determined-looking youth. Another slowly heaped up the fallen stones. Two more leaned on their tools, observing. Another, clearly the foreman, squatted in the shade directly in front of my gate, smoking and watching the others intently. Just minutes into the project, the usual Indonesian labour protocol of at least one watcher for each person actually working was already in place.

After the foreman had to move three times when I emerged from my gate, he graciously borrowed some concrete blocks from my garage and stacked himself a little bench so he could watch the proceedings in greater comfort.

Conversations over ensuing weeks revealed that the temple was a private one, not owned by the banjar but by the Gusti caste. It served about 70 families and was only used every six months. The decision had been taken to build a small kitchen and create a few parking spaces for motorbikes. There was not any land to build on so, with great initiative, the workers were taking down the bank in order to create a few metres of actual real estate.

A foreigner might torment herself with issues like, "Why would I start this job at the beginning of the rainy season? Won't this cause a lot of inconvenience in such a narrow lane with so much traffic from the two nearby schools? Where on earth will we store all the building materials?" The foreman did not distress himself with such trivial matters. "Bongkar," he intoned from behind his cigarette. And they did.

Stones and broken concrete were piled high, and an old truck came and took them away. Then the two guys who were actually working began to take down the earth bank, watched by the rest of the team. The rains began. The lane ran deep in mud. Another truck came, was filled with wet dirt, and returned several more times until a narrow strip of flat land became visible.

Now, this little project was not only taking place immediately opposite my front gate and garage, but within 20 meters of an elementary school on one side and a high school on the other. The lane at this point, when unobstructed by building materials and parked motorcycles, was a shade under four meters wide. Even a small impediment stops traffic and the construction was taking up quite a lot of limited street space. Only when it became clear that the truck delivering rebar could not approach the site because of a pile of recently acquired concrete blocks was stacked in the middle of the lane was it decided to move the concrete blocks slightly. Then everyone went home for about two months.

At intervals, trucks would arrive and decant building materials. The meter of flat space immediately in front of my garage became the storage area for sand, gravel, cement, concrete blocks and wood. I couldn't take my little car out into the lane without driving over a pile of something. But it soon became the new normal to back and fill three times before being able to exit the garage. Good for the shoulders.

It was still raining when a truckload of gravel was dumped directly in front of my car. This was a little inconvenient as I had a meeting to attend but luckily Wayan Manis arrived in time to take me on the back on her bike. By the time I came home the gravel had been moved and Phase Two was well underway. A further chunk of wall was being demolished and I learned that the project was being expanded. The team went into overdrive. Now there were four men working and only three watching. A cement mixer appeared in front of my garage, making my exit even more problematic, and the foundation was laid. Walls began to rise.

At this point my landlord and neighbour Pak Mangku caught the building bug. He decided to construct something above the shop in front of his compound directly across the street from the gate of the high school. Soon trucks were dumping bamboo scaffolding and building materials there too, and a short stretch of lane remained impassable for several weeks. The neighbourhood bore this stoically, even when it became evident that the workers were dividing their time between the two projects.

By this time the workmen had colonised my garage, parking their motorbikes there, hanging their shirts on the gate and eating their nasi bungkus in its shade. They sang as they worked. They began to address me as Nenek (Granny). Just when it seemed like things were really moving along, they all disappeared and everything came to a screaming halt.

Nothing kept happening for several weeks. The extended families of 50 households, 500 high school students and 300 elementary school kids continued to navigate their way around piles of concrete blocks and sand along with usual hazards of double-parked motorbikes, dogs, chickens and snack vendors.

Every evening Pak Mangku would stroll up the lane to stare lovingly at the half-built temple kitchen. Construction of any kind seemed to bring him great pleasure. I tried to gently interrogate him about what was being built over his shop. The Mangku is a very sweet man but I have never been able to understand a word he says. Over the years I've learned to intuit his meaning or send Wayan Manis over to make enquiries. She elicited the information that he was in fact making a guest room for tourists. Perhaps there is a special market for a room facing due west and therefore very hot, over a shop and a few meters from a very noisy high school. Also his compound had no septic tank. But he was having a lot of fun watching the walls go up.

At last the builders reappeared and things began to hum along. The kitchen was no longer small; the new building was 12 metres long and almost three wide. The Gusti caste of Ubud was clearly prospering. An upper floor was added to the kitchen block and the bottom floor was plumbed and tiled. Walls were painted. I had high hopes that the project was winding up.

But when all this was finished, someone realised that the ditch draining the entire lane in the rainy season was now blocked by the foundations of the kitchen. There was also the issue of where to vent the water from the kitchen. A pause of several days ensued and there was a great deal of squatting on heels and smoking furiously while these problems were mulled over.

"Bongkar," directed the foreman. Part of the finished floor was dug up and a new channel dug around the foundation for the rainwater, blocking the lane for another week. But we are close to the end now. The workmen are tipping the last tranche of broken bricks over the wall into the lane where, one day soon, a final truck will carry off the last of the debris. And things will be quiet again, until the next project.

Only in Ubud

It's been an interesting few days.

My Pura Dalem Puri was having an Odalan, which always seems to crank up the energy around here. Sleep eluded me and I became aware of the constant feral sounds in the jungle beside the house. Then things start happening. Early the other morning I let Hamish out for his daily perambulation and there stood my landlord's son, painting my front gate.

Now, this gate was an old one from Madura. Lightly carved and studded with hand-made nails, it has been weathered by a century or so of tropical afternoons. Sanded back to expose the grain of solid teak, it displayed faint traces of turquoise paint -- the iconic hue of that era and locale.

I loved my gate. It exuded character and solidity. My Balinese neighbours admired it. Passing tourists took pictures of it. And now that lovely old wood had disappeared under a thick coat of shiny, liver-brown paint.

This young man is a little bit one o'clock, which is the polite Balinese term for someone who is a candle or two short of full illumination. Actually he had been a clever kid who'd graduated from high school with top marks, but soon afterwards his personality changed significantly. It was whispered in the banjar that someone put black magic on him. For 20 years he'd been wandering up and down the street in various states of undress (occasionally sky-clad), busy about his mysterious tasks, always solitary. He responded when I greeted him by name and smiled shyly when we passed in the lane. He grinned proudly now as he wielded his paintbrush.

He was clearly pleased with himself. My gate had been unpainted, neglected, unfinished, bringing down the tone of the street. That was remiss of me, but he would help me out and paint it. There was no reasoning with him; reason was no longer his strong suit. I closed the gate, went inside and made a strong cup of coffee. Wayan Manis arrived a few minutes later, incandescent with indignation. "Ngurah is painting the gate," she gasped. I agreed sadly. But there was nothing we could do. No one could control Ngurah; his family was afraid of him.

I retired that night in a bit of turmoil, wondering if and when I could sand the gate back to its original condition or, if that wasn't possible, at least paint it a less disagreeable colour. I was woken from a deep sleep at 0430 by muted voices and the scrape of a shovel on hard ground. None of these elements taken singly was particularly perturbing, but there was something rather sinister about the combination. It sounded very much as if something was being stealthily buried nearby. Since Hamish considered himself retired from active guard service and Kalypso was now profoundly deaf, I rose to investigate. From my kitchen I could clearly hear that the sounds were coming from the other side of my garden wall, behind the elementary school next door. Something mysterious was definitely afoot.

With Wayan Manis I entered the schoolyard early the next morning, intent on getting to the bottom of the mystery. The principal rolled his eyes politely at my tale, murmuring to my housekeeper in Balinese that her Ibu had been dreaming. But I insisted on looking behind the school and he grudgingly led the way. Then his eyes stopped rolling. A large pile of sand for a school building project had disappeared overnight. Through a locked gate.

I lent my car to a friend for several days. As we learned in school, Nature abhors a vacuum and the Balinese abhor an empty parking area. One morning I was alerted by voices and a tantalising aroma that something unusual was happening in my garage. An empty, covered and relatively clean space four metres square was just too tempting to the Gusti clan which was celebrating a major temple Odalan (anniversary) directly across the street. Six men, two long satay grills and several hundred sticks of satay lilit had moved into my garage. A few chaps in ceremonial dress were perched on the threshold of my gate, eating breakfast off banana leaves.

It turned out to be the grandfather of all Odalans, taking place just metres (sometimes centimetres) from my front gate. The lengthy and disruptive construction of the temple kitchen opposite this gate had in fact been specifically to serve this once-every-25-year event. For a week the out-of-tune loudspeaker was directed into my garden from dawn onwards as hundreds of people arrived to pray and recharge the temple for the next quarter of a century. The noise was so loud that dishes vibrated on the table. One day I couldn't get out of my gate because several men were peeling shallots on an industrial scale on the doorstep. In retrospect, it would have been a good week to be somewhere else.

On the penultimate day when the whole lane was heaving with gamelan music and prayer, a drone roared over my front garden to record the celebration for posterity. This shocking invasion of my air space sent me racing to check in with The Great God Google, which informed me that there are no rules against this in most countries and certainly not in Indonesia.

That was the week I took delivery of three baby turkeys which Victoria had successfully hatched in Penestanan. At eight weeks old they were gawky and adorable; I kept them firmly shut up in their clean and spacious coop because they were still smaller than my laying hens who had a tendency to bully. The hens were outraged. They stared indignantly at the newcomers through the wire, beaks very much out of joint, and promptly stopped laying eggs. I checked the babies several times a day to make sure they had plenty of fresh greens and water. On the fourth day I went out early to feed them and discovered that two of them were gone without a trace. The door of the coop was still firmly wired shut. I'd mysteriously lost poultry in the past from secure coops and had hoped a ceremony to placate the river spirits had put an end to it. But they were at it again. And the hens were still on strike.

Losing my rare, exotic baby turkeys was heartbreaking. I'm generally a patient creature but a week of sleepless nights, incessant noise, a drone in the garden, vandalised gate, garage full of satay equipment and lost birds was too much. I indulged in a raving, raging, full-on temper tantrum.

Fortunately no one was home at the time.

Things slowly returned to normal, whatever that is. I hired a man who spent the day sanding the shiny brown paint off my front gate. After a few months of afternoon sun, hopefully it would bleach to a pleasing muted shade again. Trucks hauled away the detritus of the Odalan across the lane. My exhausted neighbours disappeared to recover.

Then this morning I opened the gate early to let Hamish out and discovered that Pak Mangku's son had just finished painting my newly sanded gate the same horrible liver brown. Two coats.

It's been an interesting few days. May they soon be over.

Changing Times

It was a radiant morning after a night of rain as I strolled through the grounds of my banjar's Pura Dalem Puri. Beside the temple is a large paved area where the cremation ceremonies take place, and in the middle of this is a raised platform about two metres high. I perched on a step nearby and watched Pak Mangku sitting on the grass high above a praying family, immaculate in his white priest's garb. He was deep in his devotions. The rhythmic peal of his bell shed shards of sound, the brilliant hues of the offering flowers punctuated the grass. Incense smoke coiled up to shimmer away in the clear morning air. For me, this was the essence of Bali.

The bell stopped. The prayer ended, the family stretched, gathered its children and rose to leave. Just as the priest was packing up, the first tour bus of the day rolled in to park beside the platform. By noon the area would be solidly packed with buses. They leave their engines running to maintain the air conditioned comfort of the interiors; the drivers gather to smoke or they doze in the luggage compartments under their vehicles. On weekends and holidays the temple yards on both sides of the street are full of buses, disgorging hundreds of North Asian tourists who trail into town behind their guides.

A few hours later they return. I often watched them climb back into their buses; clearly they are not shoppers. Very few have bought anything at all, perhaps a cheap sarong or some fruit. Meanwhile the smoke of dozens of buses coils up to shimmer away in air that is no longer so clear. For the use of the parking area, the wear and tear on the road and paving stones, clearing the rubbish tossed by drivers and tourists, the cumulative effect of air pollution on the temple and the perpetual traffic jams at the corner, the banjar receives Rp 15,000 per vehicle. And the town of Ubud has profited by the sale of a few rambutans.

Across the street from the parking lot, a desperately needed hotel and convention centre was recently completed. For months, relays of dump trucks alternated with the buses on Jalan Sukma to haul away the dirt extracted for the underground parking. They were digging pretty deep, and there was a pile driver.

I tried to remember the location of the subterranean irrigation channels that run under Jalan Raya Ubud at intervals. One was a tributary of the river that runs north of the town and what is now the main road in front of the market. Diana Darling opined that the Dutch constructed a bridge over it in order to build and pave the main street. Kadek Gunarta claims that it was a subak irrigation tunnel carved out many years ago by Balinese farmers to emerge south of the market and run past what is now the Batan Waru restaurant. In 2009, the vibrations of heavy traffic created sufficient stress to collapse the roof of the waterway and the whole thing fell in, leaving an absolutely enormous hole that closed the main road to all traffic for months.

When researching that story, I learned from Dek that there are at least six old irrigation tunnels running north to south under what is now the main road between Campuhan and the Arjuna statue at the eastern end of Jalan Raya Ubud. Long forgotten, none of these have been reinforced to bear the heavy weight of current traffic. He thought that two or three of the larger ones were in similar condition to the tunnel that collapsed in front of the market. The run-off from heavy rains continues to widen the channels between ancient earthen walls. Heavy traffic continues to weaken the roofs.

"The collapse of the tunnel in front of the market was a wake-up call for Ubud; it's a symptom of too much traffic," Dek said then. "Now we have a reality check. We need to limit large vehicles in Ubud, not just because the infrastructure can't cope, but to maintain the integrity of Ubud as a village."

Far from being limited, seven years later traffic has increased dramatically, especially at the east end of town. As I watched the bulldozers pile tons of rich clay soil into the dump trucks I tried to remember the location of those old tunnels. It seemed to me there is one close by. All of this traffic and digging and pile driving might well be compromising its ancient walls. It was quite possible that a giant hole could devour a chunk of Jalan Ubud Raya and close down the east end of Ubud indefinitely. In fact during the hotel construction a small but deep sink hole did appear behind the wantilan. The banjar roped it off, but someone still managed to fall into it before it was mended.

Changing times.

On my first visit to Ubud in 1969 the town was a dusty little street or two amid the rice fields, without electricity or telephones and very few cars to disturb its rustic peace. We arrived at dusk just as a procession was making its way down Campuhan hill and into the temple by the river. We crouched in the shadows by the road, delighted by the gamelan and the parade of women bearing tall offerings in the flickering light of what must have been kerosene lamps. We slept at a homestay near Campuhan Bridge that was so new the little room still reeked of wet cement. The next morning we breakfasted outside on kopi susu and duck eggs beside an open fire with puppies and tiny swayback piglets underfoot.

My next visit to Ubud was in 1992. There were several restaurants by then but the town was still delightfully comatose. In those days the few phones rarely worked, which made it almost impossible to confirm return flights and necessitated noisy arguments at the (computerless) airport check-in counter in Denpasar. It was advisable to carry a torch at night because the lights would suddenly go out and the streets were punctuated by deep holes and cranky dogs.

Fast forward to 2000 when I moved to Ubud from Singapore. Delta supermarket had just opened. Ubud was still far from stylish or trendy. You lived here in its terms, not yours. This was long before cappuccino, air conditioning, swimming pools and wifi. Most of us -- expat and Balinese alike -- didn't have much money and life was slow, sweet and sleepy. Then the terrorist bombing in 2002 shook our little world to pieces. It was a defining event for both the Balinese and the foreigners living here, a loss of innocence on many dimensions.

Things went very quiet indeed after that. For several years visitors were few. A handful of tourists and Ubud's then-small expat population kept a few shops and restaurants ticking over, but many locals muttered, "Bankrupt…" as they gloomily dusted their sun-bleached wares on the sidewalk. Buses were banned from Ubud's narrow streets in those days, but it didn't really matter as there were so few tourists coming to the island anyway.

It's really been since 2010 that the world has discovered Ubud. The sidewalks heave with tourists as never before. Along with prosperity come shops with plate glass windows, a lot more vehicles and cement. The trucks and buses are a daily event at my corner, and my neighbours now sport bright green vests as they direct them. Between traffic jams they discuss the price of real estate. Their children play with iPads and work in spas or restaurants. The family rice fields are covered with villas and hotels.

I believe we've reached the tipping point. One more truck, one more hotel will tip us right over into another reality, a new identity that is neither slow nor sweet. And through the roar of dump trucks I'll strain to hear the clear peal of Pak Mangku's bell, a timeless beacon in a rapidly changing world.

Stormy Weather

I was sharing a quiet pot of tea with Kathy one Thursday afternoon when all hell broke loose. At exactly three o'clock the sky darkened, the wind rose and rain began to gust into the patio. Between one sentence and the next, our words were torn out of our mouths and the table we were sitting at was awash with water. I shouted for Wayan Manis, who was ironing in the kitchen, but she couldn't hear me for the hammer of the rain on the roof. I raised my voice a few decibels, wrapped frail Kathy in a warm shawl and began to race around unplugging all the electronics, inside the house and out (I'd once had a spectacular modem meltdown during such a storm). I grabbed and wiped dry the laptop, its cable, the lamp and my camera and carried them out of harm's way as the storm gusted through the patio.

Chiko the parrot loved dancing in the rain and I moved his perch into the weather for a bath. He screeched with delight for a while then abruptly stopped. By this time the thunder and lightning had started, and I quickly brought him in to join us in the wet patio. He was soaked through to the skin, and the ensuing crashing and banging and fireworks rendered him uncharacteristically silent for the duration.

As fast as we dropped the bamboo blinds on the north side of the house, the squalls blew them into the patio. Ornaments and vases crashed to the floor. The rain, blown horizontally by a fierce north wind, soaked the table, chairs, cushions and carpet in moments. And us, of course.

Wayan Manis and I raced around stacking cushions and rolling up carpets. The storm had worked itself up to a vortex of electrical activity that seemed to be hovering directly above the roof. Lightning snaked around the garden, immediately followed by roars of thunder so loud that the house shook on its foundations. I like wild weather but this made me sit down abruptly on a bare bench and gather Kalypso into my arms. The old dog was trembling so hard I had to hold her tightly so she wouldn't shake herself right off my lap. Hamish, the fearless one, rolled his eyes apologetically and hid his head under my long skirt. A leak opened directly over my head and I shifted the three of us a few inches to starboard. Every time the thunder crashed overhead Wayan Manis screamed with what might have been excitement or terror.

A cataract of water poured out of the roof gutter and into the pond, filling it to the brim and beyond. I feared for the fish. The lights went off, blinked on, then dimmed again. A papaya tree laden with unripe fruit cracked and fell over, scattering green papaya all over the grass. Nyoman had been diligently pushing water off the patio and back into the garden where it belonged, only to have it blow back in his face. In a break from this futile activity, he reported that the avocado tree in the front yard had been blown over.

Now, nascent gardeners from cold climates share a particular affection for the avocado. The small, hard fruits that retailed for several dollars in northern winter supermarkets evoked warm winds and exotic climes. We wrapped them in newspaper to ripen and later suspended the seeds over glasses of water with strategically placed toothpicks. Gratifyingly often they would germinate, and I know people who kept an avocado plant in a pot for years, a triumph of willpower over latitude.

I'd optimistically planted an avocado seed from a particularly succulent specimen soon after my house in Ubud was built, and it grew into a sturdy tree of over 50 cm around and 10 metres high. In its seventh year — just as the books said — it bloomed with delicate white flowers and produced fruit for the first time. I knew I'd been taking a chance, planting a fruit tree from seed instead of grafting, but it rewarded my naiveté by giving us the most wonderful avocados.

For over two months it produced dozens of huge, rich fruits, some of them weighing over 700 grams and as big as my head. I rarely had the opportunity to taste one, however, since the dogs immediately devoured most of the fallen fruit and the others would disappear in a most mysterious manner. One day the tree would be loaded with almost-ripe avocadoes and the next there would be a big pile of them in the kitchen. Wayan Manis would make smoothies for Nyoman, visiting friends would take some home and large bags of them would go back to the family compound. Suddenly I would be out of avocadoes until the next batch fell. But it was gratifying to brag about my avocadoes to snowbound Canadians at home.

The avocado has been cultivated in Central and South American for about 8,000 years. The Spanish first described it in 1518, quickly added it to their diet and later used oxidized liquid from the avocado seed as ink on their documents, which are still legible today. In 1856 avocado trees were planted in California from Mexican stock and the rest is history.

The sex life of the avocado is very complicated, as the tiny flowers can be either male or female depending on the time of day and the temperature. After trying to get my head around whether the flower is a he or she in the afternoon on the second day when the temperature is 70F, I have decided not to carry my research further. But I assure you that it's a bit of a miracle that we get avocados at all.

Losing this tree was a blow. A healthy avocado tree will continue to bear fruit for up to 200 years. Although I only had 11 years left on my house contract, I was counting on another decade of home-grown guacamole. The tree, laden with blossoms for the next crop, had succumbed to the strong wind and weather. But instead of falling across the garden or taking out a wall of the bathroom as it could easily have done, my tree had laid itself down most politely next to the house. The only damage was a single cracked roof tile.

Once the worst of the storm had passed, we went out to survey the damage. The fallen tree filled the narrow space beside the house. "Kasihan," mourned Wayan Manis when she saw that every branch was thick with bloom. She grew up poor, and hates to see food wasted. I looked at its roots, exposed by the fall. They were small and lateral, not a tap root as I'd expected. This big tree had not been well anchored for a powerful storm. Nyoman told me that avocado wood was good for nothing but burning, so I went to bed that night saddened by the loss of a tree that had given me much pleasure and food.

But the next morning found a trio of concerned Balinese in consultation around the fallen tree. One was Komang, a gifted gardener who worked for my neighbours. Komang had actually attended horticultural school and understood these issues. He opined that it was worth the effort to try and save the avocado tree, and my staff enthusiastically agreed. Within an hour most of the higher branches had been carefully removed and a system of ropes and bamboo props had pulled the heavy trunk up off the ground and buttressed it up. Every day they pulled it a little closer to vertical, and Komang came over daily to take its pulse.

The garden was swept of fallen leaves and branches. Wayan Manis took all the green papaya home to her pigs. The fish survived. The only memento of the storm is the severely pruned avocado tree, leaning at a slightly drunken angle but still bravely blooming on its few remaining branches.

Perhaps I will get a few avocadoes this year after all.

The Real Ubud Community

There's a FaceBook page called Ubud Community, which has over 40,000 members. The active membership is divided between long-term expats, newcomers, Indonesians and many observers who don't actually live here. Discussions can be lively, with old-timers sharing cultural lore, newcomers wanting to know where they can get their eyelashes tinted and everything in between.

Then there's the other Ubud Community.

I sat buttock to batik-clad buttock in a tight row of Balinese women. We were resting on a bamboo bench inside the peyadnyan --- the long, open bamboo structure built to shelter the offerings for dead relatives. Last week a mass cremation for five banjars (communities) took place here. Taking advantage of the fact that the infrastructure was still standing, the banjars were now holding a mass tooth filing for almost 300 people. In the endless series of Balinese ceremonies, the teeth must be filed before the person can be cremated, and everyone has to be cremated. The mostly young folk were all ceremoniously dressed in gold and white and being processed with great efficiency in batches of ten. Wayan Manis' teenagers held numbers 240 and 241; I suspected that I might not make it that far. Numbers 81 to 91 had just been called. It was going to be a long day.

A week ago I was sitting in this same spot, squeezed between Wayan Manis on one side and a cheerful old lady on the other under the photo of dead Dadong (grandmother). We were hanging out during the mass cremation under the pictures of the family's three deceased relatives. The stacks of offerings under the pictures included a tethered young chick which would be sacrificed for each person to be cremated. Their cheeps mingled with the usual cacophony of the upacara -- gamelans, shouting children, barking dogs, loudspeakers, ringing hand phones and gossiping grannies.

A total of 117 lembu (bulls) and petulangan (fish, elephants and other creatures) had been assembled, each to hold the bones of up to five (but never three) deceased relatives. Preparations had taken weeks, with each adult member of the community involved in making offerings, building the structures, preparing the cremation ground and many other tasks. Before the cremation the whole banjar sat up all night praying in the graveyard and cleaning the bones of the disinterred deceased. Village Balinese are usually buried immediately and then dug up again months or years later for mass cremation, which is much less costly than a private one.

Cremation day combined the noisy energy of an ogoh ogoh parade and Christmas, with each lembu accompanied to the burning ground by a jazzy gamelan and shrieking, excited kids.

After the flames died down, there was still much to do. The peyadnyan was cleansed with many prayers, the ashes of the cremated were taken to the sea in coconut shells, prayers were chanted at several temples around the regency and as far away as Besakih, the Mother Temple itself. A week later was the mass tooth filing, with more offerings to be made, decorations and costumes prepared, more prayers.

So you see, there wasn't much time left over to look after the foreigners. The Balinese are ordinarily happy to make our cappuccinos and drive us to Seminyak and clean our houses, but when a big ceremony comes around, that all goes out of focus.

Cremation season in Bali is in the months of August and September which just happens to be the height of tourist season. In another country it might be possible to spell off staff so that they can take turns coming to work and fulfilling their community commitments. But the work ethic as we know it is a very new concept here and when Bali is in full-on upacara mode, it becomes irrelevant. Even if a banjar member now lives and works on the other side of Bali, when Uncle Made is cremated, he has to be there.

It's always hard to maintain consistency in a restaurant in Bali, no matter how good the training. During a month like this when so many staff are committed to days or even weeks of ceremonies in their villages, it becomes even more challenging. When the chefs/sous chefs have to disappear for 10 days preparing for a mass cremation a restaurateur has the choice of closing -- during the highest of high seasons -- or hoping that whoever's left can manage. Sometimes they can't. Please be patient, diners. The commitment to family, community, ritual and prayer far outweighs the importance of their jobs to the Balinese during these times. That's not going to change. If you're going to live here, you'll have to roll with it. If you're just visiting, choose to think of it as exotic and interesting instead of inconvenient.

I'm very far from being an expert on Bali's culture. The longer I live here, the less I understand. My Indonesian is poor and my Balinese non-existent, so what I pick up in the village is not language-based. It's a vibe, a hum under the surface, a finely woven net made up of several hundred people who will gather together many times between birth and death. During ceremonies, the community seems to operate as a single organism .The villagers will gossip, pray and eat the same food over and over with the same people year after year. They may not like one another but as strands in the net they are irrevocably bound together even if, as happened during the terrors of 1965, neighbour killed neighbour.

Over the years I've been invited to attend odalons, dances, ceremonies in the family compound, processions and cremations in desa Singakerta. I put on my best kain (a fine old batik from Java), my kebaya and my sash to walk, pray, eat and hang out with the banjar. My only serious fashion error is my hair; mine is the only messy head in sight. I can tell that all the grannies are itching to tidy my flyaway tresses into a neat bun. Other than that, I seem to pass muster.

There's a great deal of waiting around at all these events. Everyone looks tired after weeks of preparation and ceremony. We hang out for hours: standing, leaning, lying, sitting, chatting, texting, snacking, dozing... Two old ladies nap on a mat on the ground under a table covered with offerings. To a Balinese, waiting is an integral part of the ceremony, but I can only take about two hours of this at a time.

After the last mass cremation Wayan Manis' father and father-in-law both ended up in Mas Hospital with Upacara Exhaustion. Too many sleepless nights, missed meals, too much coffee and too many cigarettes. After a few days of rest and rehydration they were fine again. The women, of course, are expected to continue to shop, cook, clean, look after children, make offerings, walk in processions, pray all night and keep their day jobs. Meanwhile, at my house, I miss my dear housekeeper. I am a very poor cleaner.

Wayan Manis and Nyoman turned up this morning for work at last, but they were so exhausted I sent them straight home again. Tomorrow perhaps we can return to what passes for normal in Bali... until the next odalon.

Definitely and Absolutely the Last House

I can't believe I'm doing this again.

Apart from the technical, labour and financial issues, building a house in Bali is a steep learning curve for personal development. It could be defined as an excellent practice in patience and non-attachment. The best-laid plans and deadlines evaporate like a puddle in the tropical sun. You may think you have all your ducks in a row and then they make a break for it and run in all directions. Materials have been ordered, permits are in place, it's the dry season, all is ready to start the project. But wait. No building can be undertaken because of Nyepi, mass cremations, mass tooth filings, before Galungan until after Kuningan and then -- guess what? -- the banjar is having an odalon.

Just when you see enough clear space on the calendar to get the foundation poured, someone in the community dies and everything stops until the person has been appropriately dispatched. The tile supplier is out of stock with no idea when the next shipment will arrive. It's not an auspicious week to dig a well. The electrician never comes when he's supposed to. Deadlines? Just exhale. After building two houses and renovating two others I thought I'd developed enough character to last through this incarnation and well into the next one. But no.

I love my little cottage in Ubud and when I signed the lease for 20 years it seemed like a very long time. But suddenly there were only seven years left on the contract. I was a robust 64 years old. My parents were 95 and still chugging along. I was probably going to need a roof over my head and a garden to potter around in for at least 30 more years and I wanted a small and simple Last House.

I consulted my housekeeper, personal assistant and cultural liaison Wayan Manis on the subject and she pointed out that wherever my Last House was, it shouldn't be very far from where she lived because she would be getting older too and commuting around Ubud was becoming daunting. Quietly she started to explore options in her own village. After a few months she announced she'd found a five are block behind the compound of a very poor family that was available for contract.

I went and had a look. It was a flat, open and sunny meadow, unlike my shady river bank in Ubud. This land would not be teeming with River Spirits, pythons, metre-long monitor lizards, green pit vipers and other visitors. It was a good space to make a garden. Wayan Manis had known the family all her life; they were humble and good hearted. The price was right. It looked like a good match. My friend and notaris Tutut drew up the contract and Wayan Manis and I listened attentively as she walked us through each clause in both languages. "This contract ends in 2045," she said to Wayan Manis at one point. "What if she's still alive?" "I'll just take her home," Wayan Manis told her. I was not consulted.

I started making drawings of my Last House. It would be small, to optimise the garden space. At least half the living area would be outdoors. It should be oriented east-west to avoid direct sunlight. It needed to be flat and walker/wheel chair friendly. Maybe it would have a big Javanese door and facade which could be admired from across the garden. I mentioned this to a friend who promptly said, "I have a joglo to sell" and named a price I couldn't refuse.

I build houses very simply and economically. I've never used an architect and after the first house Wayan Manis' husband Nyoman has been my contractor. We've learned together over the years about what works, what doesn't and how much it should cost. Neither of us had ever built a joglo before. The classic Javanese joglo is supported by four big central pillars braced on top with interlocking beams and others at the corners of the house. These bear the whole weight of the roof. Traditionally no nails are used; the whole supporting structure is put together like a jigsaw puzzle. The steeply pitched roof ensures excellent ventilation. Since there are no bearing walls, the space under the roof can be divided up into rooms any way you please. Nyoman seemed confident he could figure it out.

As I waited impatiently through Galungan and Kuningan, Nyoman tried to find a team of builders. Labour has always been a big issue in our projects because of the huge amount of construction constantly going on around Ubud; no one is ever available. Because of this Nyoman often builds almost single-handed, which means he has learned to do everything. But as the time came for the joglo to be dismantled a few kilometres away, he'd gathered a team of old men from his village. Together they knocked down the whole structure in three days, packed it into several pick up truckloads and piled up the bits and pieces on my new land.

Visiting the site next morning I was taken aback to see what a very small pile a dismantled joglo makes. A few beams, bundles of roofing struts, a heap of roof tiles and some wooden panels. This is a house?

I went along a few mornings later to check progress. The four central posts and bracing beams were already up. I sat on a felled coconut log with my landlady, her dog and Wayan Manis as the construction team trailed in for the day. All seven of them were thin, elderly and taciturn. I greeted them one by one and was ignored. Wayan Manis laughed and told me they were deaf. What, all of them? Most of them. Why? They were old. How old? In their 60s. I steepled my palms in silent greeting and they all cracked gap-toothed grins in response.

They squatted near us, breakfasting on coffee, cigarettes and jajan in the cool of early morning. One old guy sharpened his axe, gathered a spade and crowbar and went off to extract a giant tree root where the kitchen was going to be. This was his specialty; it would take two or three long days of hacking and chopping and digging to get it out. Others swarmed up the beams they'd erected the day before. These old men had worked together on construction projects in the village for half a century and could build anything from a temple to a modern villa. They'd grasped the logic of assembling the joglo immediately.

I'd been visiting this village for over a decade with Wayan Manis and her family to attend dances and ceremonies. Many villagers already knew who I was and paused to wave when I visited the construction site. Sometimes they stopped to watch the action and hold a tape measure or help bang in a marking post. In years to come we'll meet at village functions. I know the face of every person who's assembling the beams and walls of my Last House.

I even know where the old beams came from, because this particular joglo has a story. My friend's husband bought it directly from the grandson of the original owner in Java, where it was built in the mountains about 75 years ago. Every simple pillar and wooden panel radiates history; part of the roof still has the original tiles. I hope that old roof will shelter me along with any dogs, chickens, parrots and turtles as long as we need it.

Because this is definitely, absolutely and for sure the last house I am ever building.

A House in Bali

Westerners started building houses in Bali almost a century ago and since then have been melding elements from east and west in their tropical homes. But the way the Balinese traditionally use rooms can be very different to ours. It's interesting to observe what westerners expect a bathroom, kitchen, dining room and bedroom to be, what Balinese are comfortable with and what the Balinese think westerners want -- three very different visions of what makes a safe and comfortable home.

An advertisement recently appeared on FaceBook, offering a 'Nice Villa with two or three bad rooms, nice chicken and fool furniture'. Beside the opportunity for proofreading, I thought it was a fascinating window into what a local builder understood to be selling points in Bali's burgeoning housing market. There are so many elements to a house, so many expectations; it's easy to fall into the cultural chasms between each one.

(A word about nice chickens. I think that a nice chicken around the place is indeed an important feature. I had a Rhode Island Red hen named Mabel who would not only sit companionably on my lap but often produce an egg for my breakfast. Chickens that are not nice decline to lay eggs and scratch up the exotic vegetable seedlings in the garden. Not-nice chickens make excellent curry. But in this context I believe the advertiser was referring to a kitchen.)

"Balinese generally live out doors and do not place as much emphasis on interiors as we from cold climates do," pointed out author Diana Darling who's spent over 35 years living in Bali, often at the village level. Diana's magical novel 'The Painted Alphabet', based on an epic Balinese poem and offering many insights into traditional daily life, is available at Ganesha Books and Periplus.

The typical Balinese extended family compound is still built according to ancient protocols. "The compound could be described as a curled-up foetus," explains Rucina Ballinger, another 35-year resident. "The head will always be located in the easternmost corner facing the mountains and the feet in the south west. The head is considered holy and so is oriented to Mount Agung, and the ritually unclean feet in the opposite direction. The compound temple and ritual bale are closest to Mount Agung, and the kitchen and bathroom are at the other side of the compound. The sleeping and living spaces are in between."

The entire compound may be built based on measurements taken from the length of the original male owner's foot, his footsteps being seen as the microcosm of a macrocosm. The compounds are hereditary, being passed down through the male line of the family. But the land is owned by the village and cannot be sold except in exceptional circumstances. So the Balinese family compound is a tradition that will continue to endure at the vortex of rapid change.

When a Balinese builds a room or house for a foreigner to rent, he will usually adapt his traditional understanding of each room to what he sees as the foreigner's very strange ways.

Bad rooms. It's kind of a nice concept to have a special room to be bad in, either with another consenting adult or just as a place to while away a lazy afternoon with a trashy novel and a glass of whiskey when you're supposed to be doing something else. (We all have different ideas of what constitutes badness. I have already confided elsewhere that mine is eating bacon; I trust most of my readers are able to trump this with something more exciting.) And to have two or three bad rooms presumably provides for different types of badness... Ah, bedrooms, you say.

Balinese sons bring their wives into the family compound when they marry and their sons do the same, so a family with many sons will, in a few generations, have a very crowded compound. Each freestanding bedroom in the compound will house a son, his wife and their children. Here the nuclear family and any valuables can be securely locked up at night. Often it's the only private place in a busy family compound which may be home to up to 40 people, often including a tyrannical mother-in-law. Children share their parent's sleeping quarters until the age of about seven. If there's enough room, the children may have their own sleeping rooms or share with their cousins but if the compound is very crowded, they may continue to sleep in their parent's room for many years. This intimacy requires that conjugal relations be conducted with extreme discretion.

And the bedroom windows and doors will likely be tightly closed all night. The Balinese usually like to sleep in shut-up rooms which are secure against marauding spirits, thieves and other things that go bump in the night. Security trumps ventilation every time, which explains small windows that only open from the bottom and the absence of screens and security bars that would let a breeze-starved westerner leave them open all night. "Indonesians in general don't like any breeze, whether it is open windows in the bedroom at night or an open car window while driving," says Rucina. This may be a hold-over from old tradition or fear of spirits, and is often described as a fear of masuk angin, or 'wind entering'. Ask a Balinese friend for an explanation of this, I've never been able to get a straight answer.

Sleeping alone is considered very bizarre behavior. When I lived in Singapore, the local young women who worked in my office expressed dismay that I would sleep all alone in a big house. When they came to visit, they told me that if they lived there they would all sleep in the same bedroom, for company. Maybe even in the same bed. These women were Chinese, Indian and Malay, so the sentiment against solitary slumber seems to be broadly based in Asia.

Kitchens are another room viewed very differently by our different cultures. A Balinese kitchen, another separate building, is often a dark and smoky place. "Traditionally the peeling, chopping, grinding and other preparations were done on a chopping block while squatting outside where the light was better, and only the actual cooking took place inside," Diana remembers. "Even up to the end of the 20th century, the Balinese still thought it remarkable that we would have a kitchen right inside our houses and stand up to prepare food."

Balinese kitchens should have a bungut paon (mouth of the kitchen) with a traditional wood-burning stove, even if this is only used for ceremonies. Some families still use wood stoves instead of gas or kerosene. And each nuclear family in a compound will have its own kitchen if space permits; the women consider this more important than a separate sleeping room for the children.

Balinese kitchens are often kept locked up at night. "I'm not sure why this is -- perhaps because it's the women's domain," mused Rucina. "Maybe it's a safe place to hide a bit of cash from the men of the house." I know that when I built my house, Wayan Manis insisted that I keep the pantry locked at night. "Poison," she intoned darkly without further explanation. The kitchen is the first room that visitors pass; they say that any bad thoughts they might harbor will be 'burned off' by God Brahma. It's also the place where a visitor could place something unwanted, such as a spell…or poison. As time went on I forgot to lock the door at night and eventually lost the key, without disastrous results.

Balinese compounds don't have dining rooms. The women shop for and prepare the day's food in the morning and it's left out under covers for the members of the family to help themselves to when they're hungry. People come and serve a plate of food and go off somewhere alone to eat it quickly; the Balinese don't talk while they eat. They don't share our cultural habit of the family gathering around the dining table to chat over dinner. In fact, our concept of a dinner party is very alien to the Balinese. When invited to a Balinese house for dinner, all the socializing is done before the meal is served. When the food appears, people eat quickly and then go home.

What constitutes full furniture from a Balinese perspective? They traditionally sit on the floor. They used to sleep on simple beds of wooden planks and a woven mat without pillows. In the past, clothes were stored in baskets, with the husband's clothing stored higher than the wife's and women's underwear at the lowest level. So chairs, beds, tables and even cupboards are quite new ideas.

Perhaps no other room in the house is regarded so differently by our cultures as the bathroom. In the temperate west where many foreigners have roots, long cold winters make a cosy and pleasant bathroom a very attractive option. Some of us elders remember the out-houses of our rural grandparents and are very grateful for modern plumbing and heated floors.

The Balinese think we spend a ludicrous amount of design attention and expense on the little room (kamar kecil) that is seen here as the least worthy of respect. Anyone who's visited a Balinese compound will soon realize that this is the most unimportant room in the house and one in which the least possible time will be spent. Because cosmology requires that bathrooms be located in the southwest of the land, our concept of ensuite bathrooms -- indeed, having a toilet under the same roof as the kitchen and bedroom -- is considered most strange. (So, by the way, is our use of toilet paper.)

Toilets as such were unknown until fairly recently. In many Balinese compounds, a bathroom was only installed in the past few decades with funds from the government. Until the 1970s and even today in some areas, everything we do in a bathroom was done in the closest river, in genial groups. So even though the Balinese don't traditionally socialize over a family dinner, they will gather to bathe or relieve themselves in the river together with great conviviality. If there was no river nearby, other options included the closest stand of banana trees.

So Balinese, especially elders, may well look astonished when we fuss about the colour of the toilet, paint and tile of our kamar kecil. Wayan Manis continues to marvel that I use my bathroom as a gallery, so that my visitors and I have something interesting to look at while we are sitting around. Tamu are SO strange.

When Balinese build houses for westerners, they often automatically incorporate their own expectations of what a room needs to be. This cultural element often makes for very closed-in rooms that separate us sun-and-breeze hungry foreigners from the very elements we came here to enjoy. And this leads me to my greatest puzzle. The Balinese spend much of their free time lounging outdoors on cool bales, but they often don't provide their rental rooms or houses with an outside patio or porch so we can do the same.

Foreigners living in Balinese-designed houses often comment that the bathrooms are not thought through (see above) and there is no comfortable place to sit and read, especially at night (the Balinese do not have much of a culture of reading for pleasure). Stairs are another issue. Perhaps because the traditional family compound was single storey, the stairs they do build tend to be extremely steep; Diana tells me this is done to save space.

So if the Balinese think we want bad rooms, fool furniture and nice chickens it's only because we are so strange in our ways, and they are trying to make us happy.

Stranger in a Strange Land

I was on my first visit to Canada in the winter in 23 years.

It was December. My sister Robin's serious illness brought me back over the ocean for the third time since April, equipped for the winter with a pathetically thin cotton sweater and a pair of pink socks. I went from my tranquil garden to Ubud to a high-rise apartment in North Vancouver to a remote cabin in the British Columbia rainforest in about 48 hours.

I'd been back many times as a visitor but this time I was here as a care giver, living like a resident instead of a tourist, and the culture shock was profound. After over two decades of living in Asia I no longer thought like a Westerner. I related to all things tropical, accepted delays calmly, avoided conflict, drove on the other side of the road and was faintly shocked when people embraced me on the street. When I came to Canada I looked and sounded like a Canadian but my social and cultural skill sets were very deficient. "You are like an egg," commented a young Chinese friend kindly. "White on the outside and yellow in the inside." I was about to discover how very egg-like I had become.

While still under the influence of jet lag I found myself driving an elderly and very long pick-up truck on the wrong side of the road through the forest at night. Until I found a cushion in the back, I could hardly reach the pedals. Normally I scoot around Ubud in a Jimny about the size of a double bed, in second gear. Here, people expected me to pilot this huge vehicle around at 80 kph (about 50 mph for my American friends) which I found recklessly rapid. It took me several days to attain this supersonic speed.

I was house-sitting at a residential retreat centre about five minutes drive (ten for me) from Robin's house. The day I arrived I was given a very brief briefing from the outgoing house-sitter, who led me rapidly around the property making laconic comments. "Woodshed. Axe." Axe? I was supposed to chop wood? "Chickens. Water in the morning. Feed shed. Egg cartons." About 25 muddy hens glared at me balefully. "Bye." Picking up his back pack, he strode up the hill and out of sight.

The centre, which could sleep up to 20 people, was echoingly empty except for a large and lonely dog. Taro appeared to be a cross between a Doberman and a Rottweiler and was reputed to have had social issues in the past ("He's a biter," a neighbour told me after the first week.) He was the size of a miniature horse and I wanted him to like me, so I filled my pocket with treats and he soon found our relationship rewarding. I was supposed to take him for long walks in the dark, wet forest because he was a large and bouncy dog and needed to move his energy. We had been advised not to walk along the road, although the houses were set well back in the forest and on big acreages, because 'there might be problems.' So we didn't.

But we didn't walk in the woods either, because I am a hopeless coward, a total wimp and a complete ninny about big carnivorous mammals, particularly bears and cougars. The locals shrugged off the bears but looked thoughtful when I mentioned cougars. The refrigerator sported a big magnetic decal with a bear on it titled 'Report Conflicts at 604-905-BEAR' and a list of advice about bear-proofing the garbage, locking doors to prevent bears from wandering into the house and avoiding fruit trees, bird feeders and pet food near the house. The detailed house-sitting directions I found in the kitchen told me that any meat bones must be burned in the fireplace. This is serious bear country. I think nothing of flicking a green pit viper off the patio in Ubud, but bears make me very anxious. I didn't cook meat; I cooked broccoli. Hopefully, bears didn't like broccoli.

So Taro didn't get much walking. I would take him to the trail head, futz around a little and then turn back. We'd make several trips back and forth to the chicken pen. After a few rounds of this I reckoned he thought he'd been out for a while having a pretty good time, and put him back in the house. He was inside a lot because I was spending most of the day and evening with Robin in her cabin in the dark and gloomy forest.

The chickens were a challenge too. My two little hens in Bali are tame and manageable and happy to sit on my lap and philosophize during the afternoon, so I thought I was equal to Canadian poultry. But they had their routine, these chickens. My notes told me when to let them out of their house in the morning, what to feed them and when they would put themselves to bed. Sometimes this schedule did not suit me when I wanted to get back to Robin's before dark, and I would try to hustle them back into their coop a bit early. But chickens, whose thinking equipment is extremely limited, don't take well to change. It took them several wet afternoons to train me.

Although the chicken run had torn netting walls that any predator could easily cross (neighbours told me that the owner, who is Not From Here, had neglected to take local advice about safeguarding his hens from carnivores), the henhouse was very secure. In fact it was so secure I was initially unable to access the eggs or close the creatures up at dusk, wrestling clumsily with rusty catches and heavy wooden bars.

These hens refused to enter the tiny hatch into their henhouse until the afternoon light had declined to a precise angle apparent only to them. The first day I tried to herd them in at 4.10, five minutes before their usual time. Deeply offended, they scattered in all directions and I had to chase them all over the muddy pen in too-large borrowed boots, catching them and stuffing them into the hen house one after another; they would pop out again in alarm as soon as I went off after another one. The lone cock took exception to my interference and trumpeted his displeasure from the sidelines. Only when darkness began to fall did they docilely file into the hen house and allow me to barricade the door against raccoons, coyotes and cougars (bears, it seems, don't see well enough to hunt at night). After a few days of this I surrendered to their higher wisdom and lurked behind a big cedar until they had put themselves to bed.

On Bali I rise at six with the sun and get my walk in while it's still cool. Here, it was still as black as the inside of a goat at six and piercingly cold as well. There was no very good reason to get out of bed and some very good reasons to stay there, mainly to keep warm and comfortable. Once up, it took a long time to assume all the necessary garments (and this is in the warmest part of Canada, mind). In Bali I tied on a cotton sarong when I got up and that's that. Here it was underwear, T shirt, leggings, jeans, long sleeved shirt, sweater and socks. And that was just to go from the bedroom to the kitchen. Because although this huge, drafty place had central heating in places, it was permanently set at 10C to keep the pipes from freezing.

Robin was thin and weak but as feisty as ever. She insisted on doing some Christmas shopping and timed her pain medication so we could go out for a couple of hours a day. On the second trip I noticed that the petrol tank of the truck was low and Robin directed me to a service station. I noticed with a sinking heart that all the bays were self-service.

Gentle reader, I ask you to bear in mind that this was the first time I had driven a car during a trip to Canada and I had not filled my own petrol tank for over 20 years. As I stressed to Robin later, nowhere in Asia, I believe, is there a self-service petrol station. It's all about creating employment, remember.

So I pulled up to the pump with some trepidation. I found the appropriate orifice, managed to get the gas cap off, picked up the cold nozzle and pushed it into the hole (forgive the technical jargon). I pushed the trigger, but nothing happened. Then I noticed that you had to select what flavour of fuel you wanted. I picked the middle flavour, pushed its button and a bell chimed. I pushed the trigger again. Nothing. Then I noticed that you were supposed to put a credit card into a slot. We had cash. (For some reason people in British Columbia never carry cash, even paying for cups of coffee with debit cards; real money is considered eccentric). I went into the warm station where the attendant took the money. Back outside, where it was now raining, I pushed the nozzle into the hole again. Pushed the trigger again. Nothing. Aha, I had to select the flavour again. I did, the bell chimed and I pushed the trigger. Nothing.

I was getting rattled. The attendant came to the doorway and shouted, "The black one!" What? Robin rolled down the window and explained that I was using the red nozzle instead of the black one. I replaced the red one and picked up the black one, pushing it in the hole. Pulled the trigger. Nothing. Oh yes, I had to select the flavour again. The bell chimed, I pushed the trigger and petrol splashed all over my left leg; I had not pushed the nozzle in far enough, apparently. I kept pumping until it shut off automatically, registering 14.7. But I had given the attendant $20! Robin, whose medication was wearing off, told me to go in and ask her. The girl, looking at me most peculiarly (after all, I looked Canadian, talked Canadian... how was she to know I was an egg?) told me that my $20 had bought 14.7 litres of petrol. I indicated my petrol-splashed leg. Her eyes widened and she exclaimed, "Wow, I didn't know it was possible to do that! Don't light a match."

I slunk back to the car and drove off with as much dignity as I could muster, with the windows down to prevent us from being asphyxiated. We were parked across the highway in front of a store when I noticed that I had not replaced the cap. So I had to run through the rain through four lanes of traffic to the petrol station, find the cap and run back to the car. Then I took Robin home and we both had a lie-down. I am not making any of this up, by the way.

Often, as I lay in my toasty bed in the morning trying to persuade myself to get up, dress and walk through the frigid darkness to feed the chickens, I wondered about the people who colonized this area a hundred years ago (it's called the Sunshine Coast, which is very misleading). They must have been hardy Scots indeed. Although it's only 90 minutes north of downtown Vancouver it feels like the middle of the wilderness. And it's a very long way from Bali.

A Lesson in Cherishing

In contemporary western culture we can talk about anything. Sex, drugs, sex on the rug with drugs, PMS, bizarre fantasies, snoring… anything goes. Except that last taboo, the subject most people decline to acknowledge at all. Our own mortality.

Death is the last taboo in our culture. Most people don't want to think about it, talk about it or prepare for it. But popping our clogs, falling off the perch, passing over or whatever you call it at your house, dying is not optional. Fenced into a dark corner of our daily lives, we decline to engage it. So when it slips through that fence and manifests in our reality we have no tools, no terms of reference to deal with it. One day it comes and sits beside us and will not go away. We have to acknowledge it then, and learn to walk with it.

My little expat community in Bali has an unusually high mortality rate. I've lost count of the friends and acquaintances who have checked out on my shift, many from cancer and some long before their time. I've shared that journey with some of them over the years, trying to provide whatever they needed -- listening, cooking, giving Reiki sessions or just holding the space for them.

Then, less than a year ago, my younger sister was diagnosed with pancreatic cancer. Some people do well with the major surgery that's sometimes offered for this illness, and win years of good-quality life from it. Robin was not one of the lucky ones. Since the surgery in April she'd been in constant pain and unable to eat.

I went to Canada in winter for the first time in over two decades and spent a few days with Robin in her forest house on the BC coast before the whole family traveled up from the city for the holiday. On Christmas Day Robin collapsed and we rushed her to the local hospital. She had a life-threatening infection and was evacuated by air immediately to the main hospital in the city. We followed by ferry the next day.

The next two days in the Step-Down Unit were tense; nurses poured platelets and antibiotics into her veins until she was strong enough to have a life-saving procedure. Beth, my other sister, and I stayed with her constantly and over those two long nights she grew increasingly weak; we thought we would lose her then. After the procedure she was moved to another room on the noisy, busy surgical floor. A constant stream of doctors, nurses and technicians interrupted her rest to poke more needles into her or wake her up to take her blood pressure.

Doctors began to talk about moving her to the Palliative Care Unit, but she resisted. The words Palliative Care bring dread to most patients and their families. This is the end of the line, no more pretending that things might change for the better, that there still might be a happy ending. Coming to terms with a move to the PCU means a major shift in our thinking.

But when Robin did agree to go, we found the best-kept secret in the hospital. Rather than being a place of darkness, the PCU was a wonderful haven of quiet and compassion. The rooms were private and bright. Patients were not bothered every four hours for their vital signs any more; as long as they had some, no one cared what the numbers were. Blood tests became infrequent. Whenever possible, IV lines were removed. The nurses had time to sit and chat.

Ironically, there's a lot of competition to work on this floor "because there is so much love here," as one nurse told me.

The bottom line in the PCU was keeping patients comfortable, and that meant all the morphine they needed, whenever they asked for it. Visitors were welcome 24/7 and if they brought well-behaved pets and a bottle of wine, so much the better. Beth and I took turns staying in Robin's room with her, sleeping on a cot by her side, trying to tempt her to eat, talking quietly in the middle of dark nights, sharing tears and laughter, holding the space. As the weeks went by we filled the room with books and flowers and our own energy. It became a sanctuary within a sanctuary, a place of deep intimacy. There was a lot of turnover on that floor, of course, and when we heard the gurneys pass the door to pick up the shells of people who no longer needed them, we made dark jokes. It helped.

There were nights when Robin spent hours kneeling beside the bed with her head on the mattress because it was the only position that offered any relief from the pain. I would go to the nursing station to beg for more morphine, and the nurse would give me a hard, brief hug before going off to fill up the syringe. It is so hard to watch a loved one suffer, and I talked to people on that floor who had been nursing their husbands and wives for two or three years. How do they do it? After three weeks Beth and I were physically and emotionally exhausted.

The PCU was the place between – a safe, respectful, comfortable place of transition where patients and their families and friends could come to terms with their new reality. It made me think how ironic is was that people had to get this sick to escape from the noise and chaos of the rest of the hospital and come to this peaceful haven, this secret floor that no one knew about unless they had a loved one there.

And it made me think of how we save things up, put things aside for later, thinking that there will always be plenty of time. As John Lennon observed, life is what happens when we're making other plans. Those last few weeks were a lesson in cherishing. Treasure your health and your loved ones. Time is precious. We should hug people often and tell them we love them, spend our love instead of saving it. Love earns a lot more interest when it's out in the world.

Robin was transferred to a hospice in her town of Sechelt, tenderly cared for by nurses who had often walked with death. Beth and I were with her every day. Her journey ended there a month later. We had learned to cherish every step of it.

Bring on the Dancing Girls

It was early autumn in Vancouver. I was caring for my father as he recovered from a stroke. Was I imagining it, or were there a lot more older people proudly sporting silver tresses these days? In their serious trainers they jogged along the sea wall, cycled in the parks and hiked the steep mountain trails around the city. If you called them middle-aged to their faces, they'd thump you with their insulated stainless steel drinking bottles. But according to statistics, that's the demographic. And I was in it.

At least, it used to be called middle age. But as Baby Boomers starting blowing out ever-larger infernos of candles on their birthday cakes, the terminology had to change. It was our generation that altered the face of marketing, after all. So it's Elderhood now, or Silver Seniors or Adult Lifestyle.

What is middle age, and what is elderhood? Who draws that line in the sand? When I was 20, 65 was definitely old. Now that I'm there, I'm redefining the term because it can't possibly refer to me.

My parents are 96… now, that's old. At 90, my mother acknowledged that she should be making concessions for her advanced years. So she stopped driving after dark and limited herself to two glasses of sherry before dinner. I hope I'll have as much sense when I'm her age.

We Boomers take it for granted that we'll be active and independent until we drop, probably in the middle of a salsa class. The ads in Canadian retirement magazines reflect this, featuring real estate in vibrant retirement communities, active vacations and financial advice along with the walk-in bath tubs and high fibre supplements. There are no little old ladies on the covers of these magazines; the cover girls may have a few interesting wrinkles, but they are full of piss and vinegar. And they're not in the kitchen showing off their pies, either… they're scaling vertical rock faces or nonchalantly steering a sailboat under a full-bellied spinnaker.

When East meets West over the age of 60 in Bali, there is a sometimes entertaining misalignment of expectations. Generally speaking Asians revere age, equating it with wisdom. They expect elders to sit dozing in the sun and let the younger generation take over. Old Ibu who runs the warung near my house is my age, although she looks about 80. She's had a hard life, with lots of kids and heavy lifting.

No way is Old Ibu dreaming of taking up sky diving. She enjoys her slow days on the wooden bench of the warung, chewing the fat with the neighbours, selling little glasses of strong coffee and packets of stale snacks as her latest grandchild dribbles on her knee. That's how old age should be.

Not only are the experiences of growing old in the East and West very different but now we have a third dimension -- westerners who have retired to Bali and plan to stay here until the end. We might as well pop our clogs in a salsa class in Ubud as one in Toronto. In Indonesia people are officially categorized as geriatric at 60 -- not just Indonesians but we foreigners, too. So why don't we act our ages by local standards?

Since I stopped colouring my hair a couple of years ago, I've noticed a definite shift in the way my Balinese neighbours perceive me. When I moved into the banjar 15 years ago I was just another tamu. They gradually got used to me, the kids and dogs all grew up knowing who I was and stopped noticing me. But now that my silver hair proclaims my elderhood, the community suddenly seems to regard my daily activities with amazement. Wow, she still drives! She still hauls sacks of mulch down the lane! She still storms into the high school across the street to complain about motorcycles blocking her car! At her age! There are big smiles and nods of approval when I stride out for my morning walk. "Where are you going?" they ask. "To Kintamani," I reply. "Still strong," they marvel. Good grief. Five years ago when I was still hitting the henna, I was invisible. Now I'm the geriatric phenomenon of Tebesaya.

A few weeks ago when I was trimming the rampant vines around my gate a very old, bent lady on her way to the temple stopped beside me. I have been seeing and politely greeting this lady for over a decade now, and she has always walked past without acknowledging me. But on this day she stopped and peered at me for a long time through rheumy eyes.

"You're still here," she stated at last. It occurred to me that for these older Balinese who live all their lives in the same compound on the same street, we restless tamu must seem as transient as wild birds. Yet here I was 15 years later, silver-haired now, still trimming the vines around my gate. She indicated herself with a fragile old hand. "Ketut," she introduced herself. I told her my name and we both ritually touched our hearts. Ketut flashed me a brief two-toothed smile and moved on. That small moment felt very profound; I had finally become an official resident of my street.

Bali is in many ways a wonderful place to be an elder. Most Balinese are naturally gracious and gentle. Because they live in extended families, there are often elders in the compounds and everyone learns to deal with them. For years Susan's husband who had advancing Alzheimer's lived in a little cottage near Ubud with his carers. They were endlessly patient as they took him for walks and to the beach, administered his medication, fed and watered him. His quality of life here was light years ahead of what it would have been in an institution in the west. He even had a dog.

On the other hand, Ubud's physical environment is fairly dodgy for our growing population of foreign elders. The shattered sidewalks are not exactly friendly to walkers or canes. Imagine the bleached bones of fallen seniors among the discarded offerings in the storm drains after they pitch down through the gaping holes under their unsteady old feet. Many more will be mown down by 12 year olds riding three-deep on speeding motorcycles with hand phones plastered to their ears. Still others will tumble from the ubiquitous steep, asymmetrical stairways which never have hand rails. Further hazards will undoubtedly take their toll on expat elders as we stagger around town in our dotage.

But stagger we will, because we're already independent old cusses and things like that don't change. Bali is in our bones. We've built houses, planted gardens. Many of my expat friends in Ubud are in their 60s, 70s and even 80s. They are sharp -- miles ahead of me technologically with their iPads and apps. They drive their own motorbikes or perch confidently on the back behind their drivers. They travel to exotic destinations, are accomplished in their fields and debate articulately on a wide range of subjects.

Many of us have been in Bali a decade or two or three. We've made lives here doing what we love in communities where the kids know our names. Sometimes we're a little slow in performing reality checks. Recently two of my friends fell and stubbornly walked around in great pain for a couple of weeks, refusing to believe they were actually old enough to have broken their hips.

So we're graying in our own special way, here in Bali. For seniors in Canada, life is largely orderly, safe and predictable. Balinese elders are usually part of an extended family and, in a very different way, their lives are also orderly and predictable. We expat seniors in Bali are forging a new path, seeking balance between our unusual (some would say eccentric) lifestyles, the local culture, dance classes and local medical care. People who choose to grow old in developing countries are not fearful by nature, but it's nice to know that we can get a shiny new hip or a stent or two right here in Denpasar these days. And if we fall down, the nice folks from the local clinic will be right around to pick us up and dust us off. They know who we are.

My father dozed heavily in his chair. We'd had an exciting day, with two leisurely walks and several chats, including a technical one about the origin of radar. Suddenly he spoke clearly in his sleep. "When will the dancing girls arrive?" he demanded.

When indeed?

The Smallest Room

One of the delights of living in Bali is the opportunity to build a house. This is beyond the wildest dreams of most of us and still would be for me if I hadn't arrived before land prices spiraled heavenward. Unconfined by pesky building regulations we can and do climb right out of the box when designing unique abodes, with sometimes mixed results.

When I built my first house here in 2002 I had, of course, no experience and an architect was not in the budget. So yes, errors were made. For example, I never thought about how people would enter the house or where they would sit when they got there. There is still no proper front door. Visitors used to come in through the kitchen but passing the parrot, who is socially unreliable, became so hazardous that I eventually opened up the wall further down and out of harm's way.

Once inside, there is no living room. One guest fits nicely sitting on the daybed with me along with the tea tray, but more company requires sitting around the dining table, which is cosy but unorthodox.

Wayan Manis, already my trusty housekeeper, raised no eyebrows at these eccentricities. Balinese compounds are built according to strict protocols with each building having a dedicated function. We foreigners were on another planet as far as housing design was concerned.

Balinese bedrooms are usually tightly closed up at night, doors and windows secured against wandering ghosts and the dreaded and mysterious masuk angin. Balinese houses don't have dining rooms. The food for the day is purchased and cooked early in the morning and left under covers; the family members help themselves when they're hungry, often alone. And there's no living room as such in a Balinese compound. Several generations live together and there are numerous porches, bales and steps where people hang out, sitting on the cool tile floors.

So our concept of having everything under one roof is already a little odd. But to the Balinese our bathrooms are the strangest rooms in our homes, not just in placement but in the amount of thought and money we put into designing the smallest room. We spend so little time there, and its function is so inherently distasteful. And my decision about the colour of paint and tile in my bathroom would be beyond superfluous for the 63 million Indonesians who have no bathroom at all.

Because bathrooms in the west tend not to be very interesting, in Bali we often see the bathroom as a blank slate for our creativity. I know that in Canada all interiors are invariably painted some shade of beige, possibly decreed by an Act of Parliament. Bathrooms, especially in apartments, are windowless, unventilated and colourless. For many of us, designing a bathroom in Bali inspires our imagination. Granted we only spend a few minutes a day there, but at least they could be interesting minutes.

Why have a porcelain basin when it could be terracotta, glass, granite or petrified wood? Why settle for a ho-hum tile or plastered wall instead of bamboo, stone or pressed glass? In fact, why have any enclosure at all, when we can celebrate the lush tropical environment with open walls and roofs, allowing easy access to transient reptiles and burglars? Some folk even have bathtubs, although I have never understood the charm of sitting in hot water in this climate.

I probably had more fun designing my bathroom than any other part of the house. It has lots of light and ventilation, the walls are pale pink, the towels dark rose and the countertop is rosy marble.

Because I don't have a living room as such, I've turned the bathroom into a small gallery. Since people are going to sit there thoughtfully, they might as well have nice things to look at. So I've hung the walls with a Rajasthani portrait, winsome farmyard paintings and prints and an old silk kimono. Glass shelves hold objets d'art and the toilet roll holder is a carved wooden lizard. It's a pleasure to sit there, if I do say so myself.

Pig Tales

Pork has been on the menu in Bali for a long, long time. The Hindu Majapahit began moving into Bali from Java in the 14th century, bringing their culture of pig rearing and consumption with them. But the prehistoric Balinese had already been using the sharpened bones of wild pigs as tools for millennia and presumably enjoying roast pork when it could be had.

In recorded history the Balinese have always kept and eaten pigs. This affection for all things porcine thrives at every level of Balinese society. Pigs are killed to mark ritual occasions. You don't see much of it Seminyak, but out here in the country it's common for families to keep a pig or three at the back of the family compound. When I first came to Bali in the late 1960s, these were black, swayback pigs, probably introduced from China or Vietnam long ago. Now the swayback Bali pig is rarely seen, replaced by the meaty white Australian hybrids. When pumped with antibiotic-laced chemical feed to fatten them quickly, these pigs can balloon up to 150 kg in four or five months. It takes a naturally fed pig six to eight months to attain 125 kg.

My staff, who are in the pig business in a small way, turn up their noses at chemical interventions. Why would you pay good money for commercial pig food when you can feed them for free on banana trunks, rice bran and sweet potato leaves? And there's a growing market among chefs here for chemical-free pork, so their pigs sell for a premium. One five star hotel near Ubud buys three or four a month. Wayan Manis has a special kitchen in the compound where she cooks up their daily porridge (with a little salt for flavour). After dinner they enjoy a bath and sometimes a brief massage. "Pig spa," she explains.

Before the island became so prosperous, meat was a luxury. Wayan Manis tells me that when she was growing up, all the rice her family grew was sold for badly needed cash. They ate sweet potatoes for carbohydrate, greens from the fields, tofu, eggs and sambal. When rice was eaten it was mixed with sweet potato or corn to make it go further. For many Balinese, the pig that was slaughtered every 210 days for Galungan and Kuningan may have been the only meat they tasted. In the poor areas of East Bali, this is still true.

Galungan is not a good day to be a pig in Bali. Preparing the pigs for ceremonies is a convivial neighbourhood affair. The men wake in the early hours of the morning, dress in ceremonial clothing and gather to slaughter the pigs. They then sit around for hours companionably chopping meat, spices and other ingredients into microscopic pieces for lawar.

Lawar is the ritual dish of Galungan. To make lawar, finely chop boiled young jack fruit, long beans, papaya and roasted coconut and add to spicy minced pork that has been roasted in a banana leaf over coals. There are as many recipes for lawar as there are men who make it. It takes years of experience to add the exact proportions of fried garlic and shallots, a paste of at least 15 spices, fried shrimp paste, hot chilies, kaffir lime leaves and juice and salt. Sometimes fresh pig blood is added (red lawar). It's all mixed thoroughly with bare hands.

Making lawar is men's work. The delicacy is ready to eat early in the morning and everyone sits down to consume it while it's fresh. Any leftovers are immediately given away or packaged in banana leaves and steamed. Babi guling is another iconic menu item. A whole young pig is stuffed with herbs, spices and aromatic roots and spit-roasted over an open fire until golden. Then there are blood sausages, satay and stewed pork. Nothing is wasted.

So where do all these piggies come from? There's an unusual niche business in providing stud services for Bali's pigs. It is not uncommon, while driving Bali's back roads, to spot a singular spectacle by the roadside ahead. This proves to be an enormous white boar, huge testicles swinging, being led with a bit of string tied around its neck to a romantic interlude. It seems that the Balinese are happy to use artificial insemination for their cows, but many prefer to make piglets the old-fashioned way.

The string around the neck is symbolic. He has no desire to run away. This is one very contented pig; life is not boring when he's boaring. His career as neighbourhood stud may continue for a decade. (Eventually, of course, he will end up as lawar.) It's a busy life, what with having to walk to two or three heavy dates every day, share a tender moment with a sow and then walk home. Some boars are provided with transportation. I was told that this is to conserve their energy for the passionate encounter to come.

When is a lady pig ready for love? Everyone I spoke to had a different suggestion. She would lose her appetite. She would vocalise. Interesting things would happen under her tail. She would become aggressive. Whatever the signs, when the time was right a single visit from the stud for hire was sufficient to eventually bring 10 – 15 piglets into the world. They are usually sold at about 3 months of age because it's hard to feed so many pigs as they get bigger. I'm still trying to persuade my staff that a pig needs to dig in the dirt, but the Balinese culture of closely confining pigs and cows (while letting dogs and chickens roam around any old where) is hard to overcome.

A few years ago I kept pigs myself. Remembering my first visit to Ubud in 1969 and the charming little swayback piglets that trotted freely along the dirt lanes, I asked Nyoman to find me a couple of traditional Bali pigs. This turned out to be quite a challenge but eventually he located some in Karangasem and brought them home. They were 6 weeks old, the size of puppies and quite enchanting.

We'd prepared a big, shady paddock for them at the back of the garden. They immediately escaped through the fence. Small as they were, they were already very strong, determined and extremely hard to catch. During their brief spell of freedom they managed to plow up the entire vegetable garden. We parked them in a disused aviary while constructing a wall of cement blocks. They escaped again. We redesigned the gate so they couldn't push it up with their snouts. Finally they resigned themselves to captivity.

I'd done some research on sway back pigs, of which these were a variety, and was looking forward to developing a relationship with them. Pigs are said to be as intelligent as some dogs, but if this was true it was soon clear that inter-species bonding was not on their agenda. In fact, they had a very short agenda with just one word on it. That word was FOOD.

Now my dogs, my hens and some of my friends have a strong focus on food, but they are still glad to see me even when I turn up empty-handed. Not these girls. They would scan me with their disturbingly intelligent little eyes and if I was not bearing a pail of scraps from the Bali Buddha kitchen, I was invisible. When they were still small I would take a cup of tea into their paddock some afternoons for a visit, hoping to befriend them. But once they'd established that there were no bagels in my pocket they would ignore me and go back to uprooting all the trees we had planted to provide shade for them. Their pretty paddock looked like a bomb site in a week.

I tried hard to find them attractive and engaging but they would not meet me halfway. These pigs did not want to be my friends. All animals are charming when they are young, but mine quickly outgrew any appeal on their single-minded mission to become eating machines. Pigs, like people, will keep putting on weight if they keep eating. After a few months even Wayan Manis was afraid to go into the paddock with them.

Although sadly lacking in character and affection, I must admit that the pigs did not smell. In fact they were very careful about doing their business in a far corner and covering it with leaves. What did smell was the leftover food. A pig is not a dainty feeder. Towards the end of our time together I would approach the pen with two heavy buckets of scraps, quickly tip them out into the trough and immediately retreat. The girls, now huge, would lunge right into the trough and snap viciously at each other over favoured morsels (they did not like each other very much, either). Inevitably some food would be trodden into the mud, where it soon began to stink.

I was surprised to learn that humans and pigs share 83% to 94% of their genes (depending on which gene you are comparing) compared to 99% for chimpanzees. Pigs and humans are both omnivorous mammals that gain weight easily and are susceptible to the flu. Somehow we evolved to be at the top of the food chain. And thank heaven for that.

The Geography of Loss

One sunny Friday afternoon in August, we released our friend H to the sea.

Prayers, fragrant flowers, his ashes and his favourite hat whirled briefly in the wake of the little boat off Sanur, then dispersed to become part of the great ocean that touches all shores. Only two weeks before he'd been his funny, kind, irreverent self. Then, with a terrible suddenness, he was no longer there. The lapse of time from his first complaint that he didn't feel well until that last ambulance ride was less than two hours.

A lot of people I know have died in the past three of four years, most of them after long journeys with cancer. These are journeys of profound intimacy for those of us who walk with them and hold the space for them. Whether we're walking these steep paths with anger, denial, acceptance, grace or all the dimensions in between, we have time to assimilate the reality that these people will be leaving us. We pray for miracles, but we also prepare, deep down, for their death. When someone departs as abruptly as H did, we just can't take it in at first. It's as if he'd just stepped out to Moka for coffee and a strawberry tart and would be home in a few minutes. The shock is too great; our minds protect us by only allowing the reality to seep in slowly, over time, as much loss as we can manage in that moment.

H's wife T is a woman of magnificent courage and common sense. She'd had to manage all kinds of dramas in her decades as a hotel manager, and she recognized that she was going to have to step back from this one. "Please help me," she said.

So I began to move through the uncharted territory (to me) of a foreigner's final journey in Bali. Feelings aside, the bureaucracy had to be dealt with; a call to the consul seemed appropriate. A few minutes after I finally got through (gentle reader, I advise you not to expire on a weekend) someone rang me back with the phone number of Antar Bangsa Funeral Service. Over the next few days I found that Agus, the young man from Antar Bangsa who managed all the arrangements, was a rock in turbulent waters. He knew exactly what had to be done and did it quietly and efficiently. He'd been through this many times, and knew that it took time to assimilate catastrophic loss and make practical decisions. Heaven forbid that you will ever need him, but put this number in your phones right now -- 0818565110. Agus' English is excellent, which was a good thing because I suddenly seemed to forget every word of Indonesian I ever knew.

A few hours later the Department of Foreign Affairs in Ottawa called to obtain H's full name and birth date, and the population of Canadians in Indonesia officially declined by one great guy.

The first response team from Toya Clinic had arrived very quickly with a defibrillator and monitoring equipment, and took him away in the ambulance. They were as devastated as we were when H checked out. Later, when T tried to pay them, they kept telling her to take her time. Nor did Agus press for payment -- in fact, the cremation and all the paperwork was done without a deposit or even a credit card number. We are indeed a long way from North America.

The process required a death certificate from a doctor, a civil death certificate from the government, a release form from the hospital or morgue and a cremation certificate (remains can be buried, cremated or repatriated). Agus dealt with all this.

I made a few executive decisions that T was in no shape to deal with, but she knew what ultimately needed to be done. "We'd talked about this and I knew he wanted to be cremated," she told me. "It helped a lot knowing what his wishes were. No one wants to talk about death, but we have no idea what's around the next corner." She agreed to share this story to encourage people to plan for the unthinkable. So please talk about it, and get things organized. Partners and family need to know where the assets are stashed and what your wishes are if you suddenly fall off the perch. The unkindest thing of all is to leave a legacy of mess and uncertainty for your grieving next of kin.

Childless long-time expats without property, T and H kept their assets in a joint offshore bank account; they did not have a will. Of course people with more complicated lives do need a will, but they should also have a joint bank account that the survivor can access while the other assets are tied up in probate.

We all need our rituals and rites of passage. The Balinese Hindus go out in a literal blaze of glory, surrounded by their family and community. In this, as in so many things, Canadians tend to be more conservative. The Balinese were surprised when we elected not to attend the actual cremation in Nusa Dua, but the house staff did go. Agus kept the ashes until T decided what to do with them.

Ten days later we sent H home in our own way. On that sunny Friday afternoon we gathered at the beach on Sanur where these things are done. We set up a little alter in a modest restaurant across the road from the beach with framed photos amid piles of white pastry boxes (H was very fond of pastry). On another table a huge wheel of a basket heaped with flowers held a candle and another picture. H had an abiding appreciation of the female gender in the nicest possible way, so we all wore bright colours for him and sported plenty of cleavage.

We stood in a circle as Linda said a prayer and led a Sanskrit chant. Then we each took turns lighting a stick of incense and placing it in a bowl of sand in front of his picture as we made our private farewells. H grinned back at us from the photo. Emotion rose and drifted around our heads with the incense smoke. An expatriate is someone who lives outside his or her own country. That afternoon we made our own little country in front of that basket of flowers, grieving one of our own in a faraway land.

Slowly our little group made its way to the windy beach, where the carved box of ashes waited on a stone. We heaped it with flowers, then T and a few others climbed into the little boat with their precious cargo. Muscular men pushed the boat through the surf into open water, and a few minutes later H became part of the endless ocean.

When my sister died I began to realize what a deep and complex hole death leaves. The geography of the family changes forever. One day my nephews had two aunts and I had two sisters, the next there was only one. Our elderly parents are still reeling from the loss of a child -- this is against natural order, it is not supposed to happen.

The 17th century English poet John Donne wrote, "No man is an island, entire of itself… every man is a piece of the continent, a part of the main. If a clod be washed away by the sea, Europe is the less… Each man's death diminishes me, for I am involved in mankind."

This is the geography of loss. No matter whether we live in our own cultures or far from them, we are indeed involved in mankind. Our emotional continents are made up of the people in our lives, and we're diminished when they are washed away by the sea. They leave a space that only time can fill.

There's a H-shaped space in Ubud these days. We know he'd like it filled with really good coffee and strawberry tarts and lots of laughter. We're helping T hold the space that was his until time does its healing work. Meanwhile he's a curl of fragrant incense, the kiss of gentle surf on a Sanur beach.

On the Carpet

Once upon a time, many miles away and many years ago, I sat in the ballroom of the Hilton Hotel in Singapore with several hundred other people. It was my first carpet auction.

Singapore was famous for these auctions. Piles of glorious carpets from Iran, Pakistan, Afghanistan and obscure bits of central Asia covered the stage. They were dramatically displayed one by one, each more beautiful than the last, their ages and merits described. Bidding was invited. Hands shot into the air, numbers were chanted, another magical carpet unfurled. I had never attended an auction of any kind and knew nothing about carpets. But I'd just moved into an old restored house with acres of white tiled floor... I bought six carpets.

It was my last carpet auction. Clearly I could not be trusted in this kind of environment. They were all so beautiful, my hand just kept jumping into the air somehow. Finally a friend dragged me out of the room before I could do further damage.

But I loved the carpets. Each was a distinct work of art, humming with the energy of the many animals and people who'd had a part in its creation. The sheep whose wool had been sheared, the cotton farmers, the dyers, the designers, the loom makers, the weavers – all had a presence. The carpets gleamed like jewels on the floors of the old house, adding a rich dimension of colour and elegance to each spacious room.

When I moved to Bali in 2000, the carpets came too. I knew I'd be moving from a big house to a very small one and that my life would be much simpler – that was the purpose of the move. But incongruous as they would be in my new life, I couldn't leave my lovely carpets behind.

A fine carpet, gently used, will last for generations. After 16 years in Bali, my carpets looked a couple of centuries older. My house is largely open and there's no glass in the windows, so over the years dust gathered between the tight knots in volumes that my underpowered vacuum cleaner could not clear. But worse than dust were the dogs.

Dogs have a natural affinity for carpets. In the daytime they prefer the cool tile but once the sun goes down they head for the nearest carpet. What harm can a dog do to a fine carpet? Let me count the ways.

The most innocuous substance they leave on a carpet is dog hair. Of course, dark haired dogs prefer light carpets and vice versa, so the shed hair can be easily seen. Then, if the dog happens to ingest grass or bite a toad in the garden or otherwise feel that a good vomit is in order, the dog will head for the nearest carpet on which to vacate its digestive system.

Bali dogs seem to be born housebroken and accidents are extremely rare even with puppies. But in the early days I somehow acquired a dachshund puppy. Gentle reader, dachshund + puppy = disaster for carpets. It is not a breed that is easy to housetrain anyway and Daisy had spent her first months with a friend whose house had no doors, so the dog was able to come and go at will. Never having learned to ask to go outside or discriminate between inside and outside, Daisy was hell on the carpets. If I made her sleep outside she would cry all night. Our ten years together were long and pungent.

Over the years anything that could be discharged from a canine orifice found its way to the carpets. Kalypso, my Kintamani dog, became blind, deaf and demented at the end of her long life but never messed inside the house until her last night on earth. I woke to hear her convulsing on the carpet beside my bed, and will spare you a description of the type and volume of body fluids which had to be cleaned up after we buried her in the garden.

Then when the puppies arrived late last year we entered the era of bones. Puppies chew things, and in order to distract them from shoes, pillows, toes and furniture I began to provide them with meaty raw bones. We must have gone through several pig carcasses in those six months. And unless I remembered to close the door the pups would make themselves comfortable on the nearest carpet to chew their treats, adding a patina of blood, sinew and marrow to the mix.

Of course all the dogs liked to chew on the fringes and the edges. Dead rats, birds and sometimes even chickens were brought into the house and laid reverently on the carpet by my bed, which saw the most intense action.

Wayan Manis and I would diligently scrub the grubby bits but as the years went by the carpets dulled in colour and their energy dimmed. The whole house was getting dimmer, really. I'd lived here for 14 years and was trying to find the energy to paint yet again, and get to Klungkung for fabric to re-cover the cushions for the fourth time. But life was busy and I kept not getting around to it.

A birthday was looming but no plans were afoot. That was fine with me; I was now in favour of only acknowledging the ones that ended in 0. A couple of friends suggested going to Amed for a night just prior to the unbirthday and I agreed to go along. We left at 9 on Friday morning and meandered lazily around Karangasem for that day and the next, sleeping at the nice little eco resort Balila Beach outside of Amed.

It seems that at 0905 on Friday a small army of friends, tukangs, electricians and pembantus descended on my humble cottage. Five weeks of intensive planning, endless spreadsheets and truckloads of materials came together in a whirlwind two-day home makeover. At times there were 20 people beavering away in my little house. The interior was completely repainted with a new feature wall, lights repositioned and new shades installed, new shelving and curtains fitted, the seating area expanded, reupholstered and loaded with cushions and the bed linen replaced with fine Egyptian cotton and goose down pillows.

I am not particularly observant, especially when ten of my friends are industriously pulling the wool over my eyes and purloining my keys. I had no clue what they were up to. I arrived back home after dark on Saturday night to find my house utterly transformed and a noisy group of smug, exhausted and slightly drunk friends finishing off the birthday dinner I'd missed. It was the most gobsmacking, mind-blowingly amazing birthday present ever conceived. My fresh and delightful new house looked like something out of a magazine. I still can't believe the amount of time, planning, designing, shopping, making, work and resources that went into this epic act of love. How I cherish the dear, mad friends from Ubud, Sydney, Arizona, Barcelona and Macau who made this happen.

The next morning I wandered the house in daylight, marveling at the lilac bathroom and mirrored kitchen. But where were my carpets?

I found them rolled up in the laundry shed. They were deemed too dirty to return to my now spotless abode. Oh, the shame. Then I remembered Farah's, an outlet for hand woven carpets in Sanginggan. Soon a nice gentleman came and took my shocking carpets to Denpasar where the evidence of 16 years of canine misbehavior was professionally removed.

The carpets are back now. They are gleaming like jewels again, their fringes white. Perhaps they are a little worn after our 25 years together but so am I. Another quarter of a century of dogs and dust will give us all more character.

Talking to Tokays

Ubud has always attracted a different kind of foreigner than Kuta or Seminyak. Until recently we tended to be the original hippies, the greenies, the tree-huggers, the Wiccans. Now that we are in the full flower of our maturity (middle-aged), our eccentricities are perhaps growing more pronounced. We don't really notice it when we're pottering in our gardens or comparing our cholesterol readings over a companionable coffee. We actually feel quite conservative when we observe the tattoos and dreadlocks of the newcomers. We assure ourselves that several decades in the tropics have had no impact on us.

Our house guests disagree. They particularly find our casual acceptance of bats, tree frogs and other random wild life in the house to be incomprehensible. They have no reptiles on their bedroom walls at home in London or Toronto. There are no loud, mysterious thumps and skittering footsteps in their ceilings at night. Their dogs never sit staring at the roof with alarm. Some are broadminded about this proximity to other species, others try to be and the rest go and stay in an air-conditioned hotel room.

A friend's daughter was visiting from England. She grew up in Singapore and is a good sport about these things. But once she noticed a very large tokay was living in her bedroom, she took to sleeping with her mother at night. I've had houseguests sit up all night with the lights on because they thought they saw a rat. (They probably did.)

I find Canadian bedrooms to be a bit lonely and sterile after 26 years in livelier climes. No creature, even a tiny spider, is suffered to live on those cold white walls. (Of course, in Canada one never brings up the subject of lizards, some of them highly vocal, lurking behind the pictures.) So when I returned to Bali recently after five weeks in Vancouver, I was happy to be welcomed by Ted the Tokay. Ted is an outstanding specimen who has been living behind a hanging on my bedroom wall for about five years. He's exceptionally large and handsome and has been known to utter his call up to 15 times without drawing breath, which other Tokay aficionadas will have to admit is a bit of a record.

On the night of my return he poked his head out from behind the hanging to watch me unpack. He must have been quite glad to see me in his reptilian way, because after a while he began to serenade me. "Toe-kaaayyy" he crooned. "Toe-kaaayyy," I responded, trying to match his throaty tone. We went back and forth like this, call and answer, for a few exchanges until I realized what I was doing. I was talking to a reptile in his own language.

I've always had a fondness for tokays, ever since I first heard one call many decades ago in what was then a quiet suburb of Kuala Lumpur. When I built my house in Ubud, I considered it very lucky that a tokay moved in the same day I did. The nocturnal creatures are very territorial and mature males chase smaller and weaker guys out of their patch and away from their harems. A few years ago there was a protracted tokay war in my house, when all the adult males were fighting for dominance. Battered warriors would appear under furniture and in corners with big chunks bitten out of them and sometimes a leg missing. This went on for a few weeks until the biggest, meanest tokay of all had made his point.

I'm happy to have tokays in the house. They eat insects, centipedes, scorpions, cockroaches and baby rats. They are entertaining to watch and guaranteed to elicit excited squeaks from first-time visitors to the tropics. Tokay romance is a rough business, with the male immobilizing the object of his affections by biting her hard while he has his way with her. A month or two later she lays a couple of marble-sized eggs; I sometimes find these adhering to the inside of a drawer or under the dining table. She will lay several clutches a year and the eggs take three or four months to hatch. When these eggs are laid in packing crates, baby tokays sometimes find themselves growing up in foreign lands.

Perhaps because of their call, tokays are regarded as harbingers of luck. Some Southeast Asians count the calls and use the results to choose winning lottery ticket numbers, foretell the gender of an expected baby or make important decisions; an even number of calls means yes, an odd number indicates no. Personally, I think the tokay just runs out of breath. Their calls are used for communication, finding members of the opposite sex during the breeding season, and as a means of defense -- they emit a hissing or croaking noise when under threat.

You may have noticed that tokays always relieve themselves in exactly the same place, year after year. If this happens to be on your coffee table you had better move the table, because they are very set in their ways and since they live about eight years in the wild it's going to be an ongoing issue.

In researching this creature, I came across a number of websites offering tokays for sale as pets, with advice on how to keep them healthy and happy and breeding in more temperate climates. As a pet, the tokay is considered the pit bull of the Gecko world due to the fact that it bites hard, often refusing to let go for a few minutes or even an hour. This is said to be pretty painful, and having a 40 centimetre long reptile attached to your hand makes it inconvenient to check your email. They are difficult to remove without harming them, and the preferred method is to place a drop of vinegar on its nose. (File this helpful advice for future encounters.) Due to its snappish temperament, tokays are not recommended as pets for children. However, like most other creatures, the tokay is shy and will never bite unless threatened.

But my research also revealed a more ominous trade. Tokays are a popular ingredient of the traditional medicine industry, used to treat various ailments including coughs, kidney stones, skin conditions and sexual dysfunction. In Malaysia, some people actually believe that the reptile's tongue can cure AIDS and that its blood and bile suppresses tumours in cancer patients. Augustine Tuuga, the deputy director of Sabah Wildlife Department, denied in a news report that there is any scientific evidence to verify these claims. But predictably, the rumour has created a steep demand for these attractive reptiles.

Catching and trading tokays has become a lucrative side business for villagers in the northern West Malaysian states and in East Malaysia, who have seen the tokay business grow into a cottage industry. News reports revealed that overseas buyers are willing to pay huge amounts of money for each reptile -- prices of thousands of dollars for specimens weighing more than 300 grams can be found on the internet. Malaysian newspaper The Star and Thai TV stated that Malaysian gecko hunters were active in Southern Thailand where they approached locals with the hope of purchasing tokays. As buyers are only interested in Tokays weighing 300 grams or more, villagers are catching and keeping the reptiles in cages and feeding them chicken livers to fatten them up.

I'm keeping all this from Ted, of course…

Chiko, the chatty Eclectus parrot, continues to expand his repertoire. He skillfully mimics my voice calling Wayan Manis and Hamish, and convincingly barks like a dog and croaks like a toad. Recently he has begun to produce Ted's distinctive call. Soon I won't be the only one in the house who is talking to tokays.

Bali Behind the Seen

Thanks to Vern Cork for the title

The River People are getting annoyed.

Their domain is the deep ravines that slash Bali's topography from north to south. These dark and mysterious realms are the crucible of niskala – the unseen dimension of things here in Bali. And it's a busy place.

The Balinese love a ghost story. When I first approached some Balinese friends to ask whether it was in fact appropriate for a tamu to write about spirits (wong), they egged me on. Several of them launched into stories of their own. My notes grew longer and my brow more furrowed. This is a many layered subject and my friends had different interpretations and descriptions. I'm still not clear about who's who.

I first became aware of the Niskala 15 years ago when I moved into a rather nasty little cottage up the Andong road, right on the edge of a river bank. I'd lived in an old part of Singapore for 10 years so was not unaccustomed to disturbances. But this was different.

A dark, goggle-eyed little face would appear in the corner of my office window, nodding slowly until I shooed it away. Things would disappear from my fenced and gated compound. The spirits were particularly fond of tools. If I was using a hammer or screwdriver outside and put it down to go in and answer the phone it would be gone when I came out, never to reappear. There was an inexplicable house fire one night.

My current house is on the edge of the ravine of the same river, further south. It's a busy place. Some nights the dogs and I watch as huge, ghostly faces rise up out of the ravine, then dissolve into pixels in the humid darkness. Years ago there were problems with my dogs until I built a wall to establish a polite boundary between the River Spirit territory and mine. We make offerings, but some of my things are just too tempting; a beautiful black cockerel disappeared from his firmly locked and snake/alu/luwak-proof cage one night.

"Everything has its own place, and in order to have a peaceful life boundaries must be clear," explained Padangtegal community leader Kadek Gunarta. "Ceremonies to 'open the land' take place to relocate spirits before building begins.

"But with all this development the spirits are being dislocated and squeezed into smaller areas. This creates an imbalance. The Balinese are experiencing a lot of social and economic tension these days, and that is surely being reflected in the Niskala. There is imbalance in the spirit world; we are taking up their space. Rivers are their highways and homes. Now the riverbanks are being built on and some villas don't even have a padma; no offerings are made. Rivers are polluted with garbage."

No wonder the River People are disturbed.

Tonya are communities of spirits that inhabit the rivers and ravines. "As a kid I used to hear them play the river," said writer and musician Ketut Yuliarsa. "They would bang their hands on the water, making real music with many notes.

"The Tonya were blamed for children disappearing. When I was young it was quite common for kids to go missing from their homes for several hours and be found wandering in the rice fields. But mysticism has a function," he pointed out. "In Balinese society there's little privacy. Sometimes people will use the excuse of a Tonya to cover up a human affair."

Tonya are said to be more active during the day. They live in villages as humans do and in fact resemble us exactly except that they lack the indentation between nose and upper lip.

Then there are the Memedi, hairy red humanoids that dwell in big trees and bamboo groves close to villages. They were also said to steal children, and parents threatened their kids with the Memedi to make them behave.

Tuyul are naughty child spirits. A friend who built a house in Pejeng between the river and the road found that all kinds of things would be broken in the house during the night, and Tuyul were blamed. A small ceremony and their own offering place in the garden placated them.

Another friend also built near a river in Tebesaya. She is seldom here and the house is usually empty (never a good thing in Bali, by the way). On her last trip odd things began to happen at night. She was woken several times with a heavy hand on her throat, and a massive teak table was overturned in her room. She moved into a homestay nearby while a balian was summoned. He told her that before she'd built her house a large tree had been cut down nearby without appropriate offerings being made, and the spirits (probably Tonya) who lived there were now homeless. This was quickly addressed and there were no more problems.

My friend next door has a huge tree on her land, and several people have seen a female spirit there. When the tree requires pruning it is done with the greatest respect and many offerings.

Then there are the Dete or Moro, which can take the form of real or mythical animals, or may resemble the carved stone temple guardians. I was told that before encountering one, there is a strange smell.

Leyak are humans who practice black magic and can take the form of animals. Wayan Manis tells me that her relative has toyed with this dangerous practice, and under the influence of the magic saw his sleeping grandchildren appear as succulent babi guling. The Leyak are associated with death; they haunt graveyards and practice cannibalism. Appearing as ordinary humans by day, they transform into flying monsters by night.

Related are the Lulut Mas, a seething pile of yellow worms that appear in front of gates or near water sources and indicate uncleanness. I know a couple of people who have had these, and ceremonies to clear them are quite expensive. Since Lulut Mas are the only manifestations of Niskala that seem to exist in the physical realm, I'd be very interested in seeing a detailed photo.

Really, it's no wonder the Balinese are so superstitious.

Cultural scholar I Made Surya told me about a friend of his who wanted to build on a small piece of family land on the river Oongan in Denpasar. Before he started he brought in a Mangku who specialised in Tonya, just in case there might be an issue. The Mangku detected no fewer than 5,000 Tonya and kindly negotiated with them until they agreed to move to a tree across the river if a purification ceremony as done. A week later when the offerings were brought (there are 216 special offerings for unseen beings), the big tree across the river spontaneously burst into flame and burned to the ground.

There are new regulations against building along the edges of rivers (Sempadan Sungai) but these are ignored in several parts of Bali. Big old trees, home of ancient spirits, are being cut down. Villas and hotels are being constructed right in the territory of the Tonya. It wouldn't be surprising if the increasingly irritated River Spirits began to take enforcement into their own unseen hands.

Gone to the Dogs

Hamish joined my household about 12 years ago. A street rescue, he was suffering a hideous case of mange which had eaten right through his skin and deep into his back. He was an agony of itches under the newly applied medication. He stank. He vomited in my lap all the way home, which was fortuitously not very far, and spent the balance of the day in a corner of the garden getting his bearings. By nightfall he'd worked his way around to the front of the house, too tired to introduce himself to the two female canines in residence. He was neither playful nor attractive, so they ignored him for days.

Months of medication, nutritious food, herbal balms and love eventually revealed Hamish to be a fabulous dog -- handsome, intelligent and social. But as he grew older and stronger he demonstrated the trait for which his mixed heritage of both Kintamani and Bali Heritage Dog are famous. He loved -- still does -- to wander.

On the principal that you can't keep a good dog down, he was impossible to confine from the beginning. It's amazing how Hamish can lift his now-chubby self effortlessly over walls and through bamboo thickets when on a mission. Neither two metre walls, locked gate or python-proof chicken yard could contain him. He magicked his way over, around, under and through every known barrier to visit his wide range of friends in several banjars.

This was dangerous enough in the early days. Now the heavy traffic, dog poisoners, dog meat catchers and government culling teams make life on the streets much more hazardous. Sometimes he stays out very late and I wake to a sharp bark as he demands to be let in (although he can get out of the yard he hasn't yet figured out how to get in again).

We've always had very strict rules about staying off the furniture which he scrupulously obeys when observed. But Bali dogs like to view the world from an elevated position. Hamish used to manifest his genetic lineage by sleeping on chairs and even the ironing board, until we had to make a firm rule because of dirty feet. Recently when I invited him up on the daybed with me for a photo, he looked at me in shock. "Are you crazy? Are you trying to get me into trouble? You know I'm not allowed up there." Butter wouldn't melt in his muzzle. Then he slunk off to leap over the three intervening walls (one topped with another metre of wire), through a dense stand of bamboo hanging over the edge of a deep ravine, into the house and onto the beautifully upholstered daybed of my dear friend and neighbour Jenny. With muddy paws.

Long-suffering Jenny has indicated in many ways over the years that she would deeply appreciate it if I would keep my dog to myself. God knows I've tried; my fences keep getting higher. But not only does Hamish refuse to be confined, he clearly considers Jenny's house an integral part of his territory which requires monitoring at least once daily. Since her floors are white and shiny and his paws are large and usually dirty, it is not difficult to track these visits. Jenny reports that every time I go out he arrives at her house within moments of my departure expecting (but rarely receiving) a warm welcome.

His territory is large. Not only does he range over much of eastern Ubud, but he's an active member of the banjar during ceremonies, helpfully clearing up any bits of meat that fall during preparation of lawar. He is also happy to finish up any nasi bungkus or other snacks which have been discarded by the hundreds of school children on the street. This accounts for his rotund profile; the roamer is also a forager. It's deep in his DNA.

The DNA of the Bali Heritage Dog is pretty special. Bali is the only repository of the most unique and complex canine DNA in the world. The ubiquitous and often maligned Bali Heritage Dog is neither a mutt nor a mongrel, but the purest of proto-canines with a distinctive and valuable gene pool. Researchers at the University of California Davis believe that the Bali Dog may be the oldest dog on earth.

Between 2000 and 2003 Dr Niels Pederson from the Veterinary Genetics Laboratory at University of California Davis led a team that tested the DNA of 3,500 indigenous dogs from all over Bali in association with a professor from Udyana University. Bali has two unique indigenous dogs, the Bali Heritage Dog and the highland Kintamani. These dogs have been living on the island virtually unaltered for at least 5,000 years and genetic research reveals that the ancestry of the Bali Heritage Dog can be traced back some 15,000 years to before the last ice age.

According to Dr Pederson, Bali's dogs are the richest pool of genetic diversity of all the dogs on the world. "This is only the true pure breed; its lineage goes all the way back to the first proto-dogs that evolved from the wolves. Their genes are highly valuable for further research." Because the Bali Dog is so genetically diverse, it presents many different ear and tail types and colour variations. It may be golden, grey, black or white with black or brown spots or patches, or brindle. Genetic testing proves that regardless of the wide range of colour and markings, all these dogs share the same pure DNA pool.

The Bali dog is a real character and the canine companion of choice for those who appreciate their unique bloodline and temperaments. They are clever and loyal; they learn quickly and are practically born housebroken. They don't seem to have any genetic weaknesses and are of course perfectly adapted to the climate.

Hamish has always gotten along with everyone, declining to engage in street fights or to be drawn into disagreements. But he is not patient with the young. I recently rescued two street puppies, something I swore I would never do. Puppies, at my age. What was I thinking? Hamish echoed this sentiment.

For the first two months he tried hard to ignore them, growling when they jumped on him and leaving the room when they became too bouncy. Frequently we'd lock ourselves into the house in the evening when the puppies' collective energy levels became too high for our elderly nerves. But I notice lately that he's more tolerant, and allows them to follow him around the garden. Perhaps he is mellowing. Perhaps he realises that he is now the patriarch and will pass down his skills to the new generation... leaping tall walls in a single bound and dragging home pig jaws. It's in his DNA. I'd better make the walls higher.

Ubud, the One-Trick Pony

When I first came to Ubud in 1969 it wasn't much geared for tourism. I remember a few home stays and the Campuan Hotel, a couple of simple warungs (this was five years before Murni opened Ubud's first real restaurant) and not a single souvenir shop. The village was strung out along a few narrow, dusty tracks amid endless rice fields. Electricity would not arrive for over a decade; at night, kerosene lamps lit the darkness and everyone went to bed early. I don't know whether anyone was counting tourists in Ubud in those days, but he probably could have done it on his fingers and toes.

"Agriculture drove the economy here until the mid 1980s," says photographer Rio Helmi, who has lived in Ubud since the 1970s. "That's when electricity arrived. Television soon followed, and the outside world came blasting into Bali. The island became porous, absorbing influences from elsewhere for the first time. "

The Nusa Dua hotel enclave was developed to accommodate growing numbers of international tourists, some of whom were wandering up as far as Ubud in the late 1980s. Not many at first—there was no beach, so it took a while for travellers to realise that the quiet village had its own unique charm. One thing led to another. Day trippers would stay longer if there were more guest houses. They needed to eat: a few little tourist-friendly restaurants opened. Tourists wanted to buy paintings, wood carvings and textiles and it was easier to open a small shop than to peddle wares from porch to porch. They were interested in the culture, so dance performances were arranged in the evenings.

Fast forward 2015. Just two generations have passed.

The charming agricultural village has swollen into a dirty, traffic-congested town jammed with guest houses, hotels, restaurants and shops. Almost every business in the centre of town and many on the periphery is focused entirely on the tourism industry. Almost every family compound has at least one member working in tourism as a driver, maid, cook, shop assistant, guide, spa therapist, waiter, villa manager or night watchman.

"Ubud's economy is very prosperous compared to villages nearby and many people have become extremely wealthy," Rio told me. "The agricultural leg of the economy has been amputated and everything now pivots around tourism. It makes the local economy very vulnerable. The pitfalls of a mono-economy are like the dangers of monoculture; one pest/problem can spread quickly and wipe out the entire crop. The Bali bomb in 2002 shut down the tourist industry for years.

"All the existing sectors are connected to tourism -- construction, architecture, shops, restaurants, hotels -- which means the people in those industries end up making the big decisions which have a strong influence over culture.

"Many Ubudites are heavily mortgaged. They buy cars and motorbikes on credit so they're very exposed because they are all dependent on tourism. This unreal bubble is getting bigger and bigger. There's no diversity, nothing else to fall back on if tourism fails. One bomb or a financial crisis could make Ubud a ghost town overnight."

Rio went on to describe the cultural erosion he's witnessed, especially over the past few years. It's been insidious, as these things often are. When I moved here in 2000 all the shops and restaurants used to shut for at least one day at Galungan. Then they started to open late in the afternoon and now they all open at noon so the staff can pray quickly and get back to work; the tourists must be fed. On Nyepi eve, it used to be mostly Balinese families gathering to watch the ogoh ogoh on the football field. Over time more and more foreigners joined the throng and this year Balinese faces in the crowd were rare. And in this hierarchical and still feudal society, young people of all castes find themselves doing the same work for the same wages. There's some thesis material here.

But this isn't another rant about uncontrolled tourism. I'm looking at Ubud's young people and wondering what will become of them. I am making some broad generalisations here, but there is definitely a trend.

Higher education is rarely considered by Ubud parents, unless it's tourism-related. There are now so many jobs in the sector that anyone who wants to work can do so, and thinking ahead is not part of the culture. Wages and tips go on a new motorbike, iPhone, or tablet because most young people live at home and don't pay rent. That, along with easy credit and the easy money from land sales has created a strong consumer society in a culture where the work ethic is a new concept.

I know many committed, hard working young Balinese with a great work ethic. But then there are the others.

Friends who have business here tell me it's become very difficult to find and keep staff recently. It seems that no one wants to do production work anymore. Kids are very selective these days and prefer to work in a villa, a spa or a fashionable restaurant, thank you. And when they get bored, or their friends get a job in a trendier place, they quit without notice. Those of us who grew up with a Presbyterian work ethic find this behaviour very strange. So does my diligent housekeeper Wayan Manis. "Lazy and spoiled," she mutters darkly.

"This is a very serious problem in Ubud," the owner of one popular restaurant told me. "No matter how well treated and well paid the staff are, they have no loyalty and leave without even a day's notice. They are completely unskilled coming in, so a lot of time and effort goes into training. But so many of them just don't want to work. And it's worse now than when I opened three years ago.

"Ubud badly needs an association of business owners to work together to improve skills and instill a work ethic. We need a system of personal references -- without them there's no way to track skills, experience and integrity. Tourism is a service industry and tourists' expectations are high. And what happens if a there's another bomb or some other disaster that shuts down tourism?"

A producer of chemical-free food products said, "Finding staff has been such a problem for us. Anything associated with farming is not cool amongst young people. They generally want a job with status, which in this tourist-based economy means a restaurant or hotel. Balinese youth seem to be increasingly interested only in 'easy money' formulas. The older generation has a stronger work ethic and is generally much more reliable."

A factory owner with 30 years of garment production in Bali agrees. "I have half a dozen jobs on offer including management level positions, but no candidates. Everyone wants to 'work in a villa'."

There's a serious lack of role models for young Indonesians. With no one to inspire them at the banjar, provincial or national level they are literally left to their own devices in both meanings of the word. I've often walked into a shop to find the serving staff all so focused on their phones that they don't even look up. (And the terrifying habit of casually texting messages while driving a motorcycle often has a predictable if messy outcome.)

So here we have it. Ubud is a town that's hooked on money with a population that increasingly regards the tourists who generate it as a cash crop. But crops fail.

Who will feed the one-trick pony once the circus has moved on?

The Art of Happiness, Bali-Style

Happiness is both an art and a science. My grandmother used to say that people were just about as happy as they decided to be. The Dalai Lama states that the purpose of our lives is to seek happiness. Back in the laboratory, psychologists and neuroscientists are trying to figure out what it is and how it works.

There's something about Bali that makes a lot of people feel happy. I'm fascinated by that. Bali is full of people who came here for a holiday and never left. Grumpy, tired, stressed-out people wake up on their first morning in Bali feeling better. A week later they are trying to figure out how to move here.

According to psychiatrist Howard Cutler, many surveys show that unhappy people tend to be more self-focused and are often withdrawn, brooding and even antagonistic. Happy people are generally more sociable, flexible and creative, able to tolerate life's daily frustrations and are more loving and forgiving than unhappy people. So we bring some baggage with us. We can change some traits by working on them consciously. But is there something else in the air here, some ubiquitous element that just makes us feel -- well, happy?

I did a quick poll of some friends to see why Bali pushed their happy buttons. The most common answers were weather, the green, lush environment, the Balinese sense of community and the absence of ageism. Most often people just replied, "The Balinese."

Weather is a big issue for those of us raised in grey and gloomy northern latitudes. Seasonal Affective Disorder (SAD) is a condition in which people with normal mental health throughout most of the year experience depressive symptoms in the winter. It's been argued that SAD is an evolved adaptation in humans that's a remnant of a hibernation response in some remote ancestor. These days winter just makes us depressed when the sun's not out. SAD affects up to 10% of people living in areas with dark winters, including me. The permanent cure? Move to the tropics.

Studies have shown that subjective wellbeing levels increase when people are surrounded by greenery instead of concrete. I also suspect that increased oxygen levels may play a role. And just being out of an urban environment with its many subtle stresses and strains is probably a huge plus.

But there must be more to it than that. I talked to professional happiness consultant Marisa who spends part of the year in Bali. Marisa designs and leads workshops on the science of happiness, resilience and well-being in the private and public sectors and in schools in Australia. The workshops help people look at their mind sets and investigate how they think about themselves, their worlds and what they can influence. "At the end of the day it's about connection with others," she told me. "Otherwise we live in a world of self-absorption which does not lead to happiness." So when people replied that the sense of Balinese community, the connectedness, made them feel happy they were responding to a very profound instinct that is increasingly lacking in our own societies.

"Social connection is the strongest predictor of happiness, that's very clear in the research," said Marisa. "People live longer, have better marriages, experience more contentment, all based on the quality of how they connect with others. Depressed people often don't have much social life."

Perhaps westerners here are drawn to the community orientation instead of the strongly individual orientation we are used to. The Balinese learn at an early age not to assert their own individuality at the cost of group peace. Some westerners see this as a negative, but in fact the urge to constantly impose our personal emotions and opinions on others doesn't demonstrate behaviours related to emotional intelligence and resilience such as impulse control and empathy. Science has traditionally looked at the survival of the fittest, at what we need to survive. The focus in the last 15 or so years has turned to what we need as individuals to thrive. Neuroscience is now looking beyond individuals and at social connections. Indeed, no man is an island. Bonding, connection and cooperation are the social glues that hold us together in coherent groups.

"The power of suggestion is huge," Marisa pointed out. "Think of all the prayer and energetics we pick up here subliminally. Maybe we sense and respond to the energy of strong extended family bonds, social cohesion and the commitment to the banjar, the immediate community, that's integral to the Balinese culture. They've learned to co-operate and get along at a deep level.

"To further explore the question of what is it about Bali that makes people happy, we should look at what we know through scientific inquiry about happiness. First we need to accept that happiness doesn't just passively happen to us but is a choice. As with all personal growth interventions, awareness is key. Some of my clients are shocked when I point out that whilst there is a genetic component to happiness, research indicates that over 40 % of happiness is contributed by intentional activities. Many people argue that this figure under-represents the power of intention, and thankfully research is starting to investigate this further. Surprisingly, it turns out that our environment plays a relatively minor role in our well-being and happiness.

"We know that having solid quality relationships and social connections are the strongest predictors of well-being and happiness. We also know that we are literally wired to connect. In positive social situations, our brains respond to other people by producing feel-good chemicals and oxytocin, which is referred to as the 'bonding hormone'. This also happens when we do volunteer work, or help others for the greater good."

How to define happiness? A combination of many factors contributes to our subjective well-being, or happiness. These include having good quality relationships, clear purposeful goals, living a mindful conscious life, (with focus on others) having an optimistic style of interpreting your world, future and self, knowing and using personal character strengths in order to being in 'flow' states, having healthy habits in terms of sleep, nutrition and exercise and having more positive emotions to negative ones. It's a mindset, a skill-set -- habits that, when cultivated on a daily basis, make and keep us happy.

Often we see Balinese sitting around laughing, chatting, and relaxed. They spend a lot of time together raising children, preparing feasts, praying or making offerings together. Basically, they're doing what is referred to by psychologists and practitioners as 'on task training', which is essentially a form of 'mindfulness' practice. In other words, they practice mindfulness daily. We know that mindfulness training leads to a greater sense of calm, lower blood pressure, greater focus, greater memory, increase in grey matter and a positive effect on the limbic system in our brains (which positively effects emotional regulation). We tend to forget that tranquility is a positive emotion, which many westerners don't experience often enough in their busy, crazy lives.

So maybe connection is at the core of Bali's magic, connection to nature, people, beauty, culture and to self. The Dalai Lama says, "I think without that feeling of affection and connection with other fellow human beings, life becomes very hard."

Indeed, people are as happy as they decide to be. People are happy by choice but they have to make that choice and cultivate it. And Bali is a fertile garden for those seeds of happiness.

Nobody Likes a Mean Duck

In my early days in Bali I kept Indian Runner ducks, the charming but singularly brainless species found in Bali's rice fields. It was my first experience keeping poultry and I soon learned that it was a fine balance between entertainment and inconvenience. The ducks were too stupid to procreate. They attempted to mate with other species, laid eggs but never figured out how to hatch them and exhibited other behaviours not likely to increase the duck population. These adventures are chronicled in my book 'Bali Daze -- Freefall off the Tourist Trail' in case you are tempted down this path.

Then I moved to a piece of land on a steep, heavily jungled ravine. I soon learned that my new home was Predator Central. Large pythons, metre-long monitor lizards and luwak/musang were frequent visitors with a keen interest in my poultry. I lost countless laying hens, bantams, Indian Runner Ducks and a couple of quail over the years.

Last year Greg gifted me with three adolescent Muscovy ducks. The Muscovy grows to be a big bird, hopefully big enough to talk back to the wildlife. Mature drakes can achieve seven kilograms and females half of that. Not often seen in Bali, these large terrestrial ducks with warty red faces were originally from Central America but were brought to Bali along with many other food plants and animals over the centuries.

Even at their tender age the new ducks struggled strongly as I lifted them out of their travelling basket. For the first few months they chugged busily around the garden without demonstrating a great deal of personality. Gradually it became evident that one of them was growing much larger than the others and we deduced that this was a male. I called him Randy, in anticipation of the dynasty I hoped he would be founding. The girls were Ruby and Roberta. Ruby was sleek and flirty, a very pretty duck as Muscovies go (if you can overlook the interesting red warts on their faces). Roberta was shy and reserved. Although the ducks were very co-dependent and always hung out together, she kept a little apart.

As the months went by the ducks' feathers took on a lovely iridescent black lustre, contrasted by white markings on their wings and breasts. They cruised the garden like stately galleons, their large bodies surging along gracefully as they consumed, one by one, all my best bedding plants. They cavorted in the fishpond and devoured the pond plants and sometimes ventured into the front yard to leave their mark in the small pond there too.

Randy grew ever larger and became, at less than six months of age, a most impressive duck. His hormones began to kick in about this time and he suddenly noticed that Ruby was a very attractive female of the species. He took to following her around the yard, more and more urgently, without quite knowing what to do when he caught up with her.

Most birds procreate with a gentle cloacal kiss (look it up). Ducks are almost unique in the bird world in being endowed with sizeable genitalia; of almost 10,000 species of birds only ducks, geese, swans, ostriches, emus and cassowaries are thus equipped. The spiral penis of a Muscovy drake can measure 20 cm. Consider how that compares with most humans. Biologically the unique long, spiral penis makes sense as it prevents any other species of duck from breeding with Muscovy hens, but the choreography and cooperative spirit necessary for successful procreation are considerable.

I happened to be present on the day Randy figured out what went where. He and Ruby were swimming in the pond, with Roberta watching from the sidelines as usual. Suddenly Randy climbed on top of Ruby, who was a third his size, and pushed her almost completely under water. It took quite a while to sort things out and they both had to come up for air a few times. By the end of the encounter poor Ruby was so weak I had to help her out of the pond with a net. She lurched in circles on the grass for a while streaming water, feathers every which way and her eyes rolling around in her head. It had not been a romantic interlude.

But it must have kicked off her hormones. A few days later she laid her first egg. We built a little hut from woven bamboo inside their predator-proof pen and she began to lay an egg every day in the straw. I anticipated fuzzy ducklings and went off to Canada for two weeks.

On my return, the situation had clearly changed. I noticed that Roberta had had a growth spurt and was suddenly almost the size of Randy. Ruby was sitting a clutch of 8 eggs and was no longer sexually available. Randy showed no interest in the other duck, but when Ruby took a break from brooding one day and wandered toward the pond, Roberta made a clumsy attempt to mount her. Aha! Roberta was, in fact, Roberto!

Randy witnessed this liberty from across the garden and charged at Roberto with his big wings outspread, hissing loudly. He chased the poor guy into the pen and cornered him there, pecking and hissing while poor Roberto tried to make himself invisible in the straw.

It was soon clear that Randy's hormones were raging out of control. He made Roberto's life a nightmare and then turned his wrath toward Kalypso, my half-blind old dog. He took a dislike to her and began to chase her aggressively around the garden, snapping at her heels. On one occasion she retreated to the patio and he followed her right into the house. This was too much. I stepped between them and raised my arms but, nothing daunted, Randy spread his metre-wide wings and hissed at me threateningly.

Within a couple of days my tranquil home and garden had become a battle zone. Both dogs were nervous and snappy, I was apprehensive and Roberto was miserable. Randy had become a bully and a thug. There was only one solution.

That is when I discovered, after many years of working together, that my Wayan Manis was too tender-hearted to dispatch a chicken, much less a large and angry duck. Pak Pasak, the gardener, had no such qualms. The next morning he strolled to a remote corner of the yard with a sharp knife under one arm and Randy under the other. Half an hour later, dressing out at an impressive 2.5 kilograms, the offender was in the freezer awaiting a special occasion.

Nobody likes a mean duck, Randy.

It took the dogs and ducks a day or two to realize that the tyrant was no longer part of the community. Ruby and Roberto began to hang out tentatively together. But she was spending less time on the nest and one morning I noticed eggshells in the enclosure. Soon Ruby had eaten most of the eggs she'd been sitting on. Wayan Manis and I agreed that her maternal instincts seemed to be out of calibration, which did not bode well for future generations.

Perhaps because of his slow start, Roberto never really grasped the mechanics of procreation. He chased Ruby around and around the garden with great determination. When he caught her he stood on her head, or on her back facing the tail. He seemed to be wondering why nothing was happening. So did Ruby. My fantasies of baby ducks were put on hold indefinitely.

But life returned to normal. Kalypso once again dozed undisturbed at her post overlooking the pond. Every once in a while I'd think of how peaceful the garden is and how pretty the ducks look among the remaining plants. Then I went back to researching a nice recipe for duck a l'orange.

Havoc in the Henhouse

What is it about fat red hens that is so endearing? They are very cosy and reassuring, somehow. As kids, we used to hang around the chicken coop at my grandparents' farm where we were pecked collecting eggs and learned the facts of life. Later we kept bantams in the suburbs until they started roosting high up in the pine trees. My sister Robin raised a flock of chicks in her bedroom closet after she left home.

Then several years ago she sent away for half a dozen assorted day-old chicks which arrived at her farm just before I did on one of my trips to Canada. Because it was cold outside, she raised them in her bathtub under a Grow Light. Since they had been shipped the day they hatched, we were pretty much the first people they'd set their beady little black eyes on. They quickly adopted us as their VIPs, hopping happily into our hands for a cuddle. Six months later, when I was back at the farm, one of my tasks was to feed the hens and collect the eggs. They were still enchanting, although now huge compared to their Balinese sisters. These were serious laying hens, weighing in at about 3 kilograms. Every time I opened the hen house door at least one would fly at me in excitement, and I have to report that it's quite disconcerting to have a large bird fly at one's face. It took me a day or two to realise that they were not escaping or attacking. They were trying to fly into my arms.

My passion for keeping chickens was re-ignited. I'd tried to keep Bali hens a few times, and had dabbled with Indian Runner and Muscovy ducks and even geese. The combination of pythons and my murderous dachshund had ended these experiments, usually in little piles of feathers. But Daisy lived elsewhere now and I began to toy with the possibility of getting a couple of chickens. Several friends in Ubud kept laying hens and the eggs were delicious.

We all have our little eccentricities and one of mine has been an obsession with designing chicken coops. I still have drawings I made decades ago in my apartment in Vancouver, never imagining that I would be unfolding them next to a Balinese jungle. A few years ago I'd tried to share my vision with Nyoman, who had created in my absence a completely unrecognizable structure; he had, of course, never seen a real hen house. Balinese chickens live in tiny wooden boxes or are allowed full liberty, nothing in between.

I spent several evenings adapting my original hen house plan to suit a couple of hens in the tropics, incorporating the chicken tractor concept I had learned in permaculture class. Nyoman was bemused, but under close supervision eventually produced a portable, 3 metre long tent-like structure framed in bamboo and covered with fine net. Security was high on my agenda, given my lamentable history as a poultry keeper. Robin's henhouse is a very substantial building made of thick lumber and the kind of heavy wire mesh they use on the cages of the more antisocial animals at the zoo; she was in bear country. I was more worried about pythons and dogs. Kalypso, although now elderly, had learned from Daisy how to run down a chicken and break its neck in a New York minute.

Two hens soon arrived in a stylish purple net bag. These were not Bali chickens, but real laying hens. They were plump little redheads with plenty of curves, resembling a cross between Buff Orpingtons and Rhode Island Reds. Wayan Manis, Nyoman and I admired their glossy russet feathers and trusting way of nestling into our arms.

But once released into the ecologically correct chicken tractor, their indignation was instant and palpable. These had been free range hens in a friend's garden, scratching in the compost and wandering at will. They were deeply unimpressed by their new high-security lodgings, even disdaining the cosy nesting box filled with fragrant rice straw. Every time one of us appeared they would race to the netting wall and demand to be let out. A few days later we attached a large aviary to one end of the pen, but they still weren't happy. "They want to be free, Ibu," explained Wayan Manis, who couldn't understand why all chickens, dogs and children couldn't just do as they liked. Where was the boundary between prudence and being a control freak, I wondered?

About this time the chickens next door started to take an interest in the exotic newcomers. Pak Mangku's scrawny hens soon began to fly over the wall in hopes of availing themselves of the superior catering. Inevitably they were accompanied by Pak Mangku's wicked white rooster, hereafter known as Spike. Spike was the avian incarnation of the Bad Boy every mother dreads will cross her innocent daughter's path. If he was a human he'd be wearing cowboy boots, smoking a Marlboro and packing enough testosterone to fuel a 747.

Spike began to fly on top of the wall that separates my garden from Pak Mangku's, beat his chest with his wings and crow loudly before leaping down into my garden and strutting toward the cage. My naïve girls gaped in awe at this specimen of uber-masculinity; they'd led very sheltered lives until now. Spike's skinny little spotted wife followed him adoringly but he ignored her, fascinated as he was by my chesty little red hens. They were equally fascinated with him. I'd chase him off with sticks and the hose and he'd strut unhurriedly to the wall, leap onto it and let loose with a deafening hormone-driven crow just to let me know he was leaving on his own terms.

Now, these chickens of Pak Mangku's had already been an issue for some time. When it finally stopped raining I'd put in a vegetable plot, started some seedlings and planted tomatoes, lettuce, beans and a rare kind of Russian kale, lovingly mulched with ylang ylang. Early one morning Spike and his harem scratched up almost every plant and spread the mulch from here to Peliatan. After a disgraceful show of temper on my part I directed Nyoman to net in the entire patch, as well as the vegetable garden in front. This made the gardens difficult for me to access but it did keep the chickens out.

Clearly the hens would not start laying until they were happy. I decided to give them a bigger enclosure, and this meant yet more netting. Nyoman rolled his eyes (he's developed this into a fine art) and Wayan Manis added the cost of the netting to our monthly cash book. I was clearly spending more on enclosures to keep chickens in and other enclosures to keep chickens out than I would pay this year for vegetables and eggs. But they are used to me now. In my small, eccentric way I'm good for the economy of local hardware stores, and I certainly provide plenty of entertaining stories to take back to the family compound. So Nyoman constructed a chicken run beside my bedroom, the girls' wings were clipped and they were set free to run around and scratch at last. They were ecstatic.

So was Spike. He began to spend all his time there, helping himself to their table scraps and sprouts and doing his best to impress them. I told myself that his presence would stimulate the production of eggs, of which there was so far no sign. Wayan Manis assured me that we could sell the eggs, if there ever erre any, to meet the cost of the feed. It could take a while to break even.

I can't recommend keeping two hens as a business model, but they are certainly pleasant company. Their thinking boxes are exceedingly small but they're very affectionate, running to greet me in high excitement whenever I appear. Often when I dropped by to check them out I find that Wayan Manis was already there, feeding them tidbits from her lunch. The dogs watched politely from outside the fence and Chiko the parrot would stroll over to have a look too. They became part of the family.

But every chicken or duck I'd ever named came to an abrupt end, so I just called them both Chookie at the beginning of the relationship. After a few weeks I broke down, though, and named them. It seemed unsociable not to. They were so very friendly, and most obliging in finally presenting me with fresh eggs every day. In appearance the chickens were so similar that I couldn't really tell them apart, so I called them Maude and Mabel interchangeably. A year later I was still enjoying their scatty, sociable presence which was rather a record given my perilously predator-friendly location. The girls went into lockdown at night, and by day I had to grab the eggs before the monitor lizards.

One can get absurdly attached to chickens. Maude and Mabel would run to greet me when I visited the pen and sit contentedly on my lap, making little clucking noises. They crowed with victory each time they delivered a new egg, then turned around and regarded it with deep bemusement. On very good days, when all the stars were aligned, they would lay two eggs each. Mostly it was one egg per hen per day, though, which kept me in breakfasts with lots of extras to give away.

These were possibly the most expensive eggs in the Republic of Indonesia, since Wayan Manis fed them fresh greens, corn, red rice, scrambled eggs (the commercial ones), powdered dried eggshells and, occasionally, chicken meat from an offering. They loved meat. (I have a Swiss friend here who feeds beef to her hens, and they are still laying enthusiastically six years later.) They spend the day scratching contentedly in the dirt and dry rice straw of their pen, accepting gifts of grubs and grasshoppers from the garden, wallowing in dust baths and busily doing other chicken things in the hours of daylight. At night they were locked inside a bamboo coop, securely covered in fine netting to keep out snakes, which was located against my bedroom window. It was pleasant to drowse awake to their inane chicken mutters at first light.

Then very early one dark night I was woken by what sounded like a feral cat being strangled directly outside my window. It took me a minute to wake up and realize that the hysterical bumps and distressed chicken noises signaled a drama that would have to be dealt with. The dogs, slumbering on the carpet beside my bed, woke and watched me grab the flashlight. "Let's go, there's something happening out there," I ordered. Avoiding my eyes, they both put their heads down on their crossed paws and feigned sleep. Kalypso considers herself too dignified for nocturnal adventures, and Hamish is conflict-averse.

The night was cold and black. I picked my way around the house to the chicken pen. One of the hens was flinging herself wildly against the door of the coop. I shone my torch through the netting at the other end of the structure. A snake as thick as my arm was coiled there, its head out of sight, wearing the unmistakable silver, gold and black livery of a reticulated python. There was no sign of Mabel; presumably she was being dealt with by the business end of the snake out of sight under the roof of the coop.

I opened the door at the near end and Maude exploded out of the coop like a cannonball. Locking the door behind her, I ran in pursuit. The frantic hen rushed round and round the dark garden with me close behind. I headed her back toward the house and she promptly fell into the fish pond with a muffled splash. It was soon clear that Maude could not swim, and I had to go in after her. Wet to the waist, plastered with pond plants and with a soaking and traumatized hen under my arm, I climbed back out onto the grass. I took a moment to reflect how difficult it was to explain this sort of thing to my friends in orderly, placid urban Canada.

Both Maude and I were shivering by this time. I towelled her dry and for lack of a better option locked her into the pantry for the balance of the night. Back in bed in a dry sarong as the python lay a few feet away behind the wall assimilating my best laying hen, I pondered how the snake had gotten into the coop in the first place. It had been designed it to be predator-proof because I live on a river bank and the wildlife of the undercliff — pythons, musang and monitor lizards – are very fond of chicken. So the walls of the coop were fine mesh and the wire doors had gaps of no more than 2cm. A snake the size of the python couldn't possibly have gotten in... but it somehow it had. In the morning it would still be there, with a large, Mabel-shaped bulge in the middle, unable to escape. I fell asleep making plans to release it far, far away.

But dawn arrived to reveal that, impossible as it seemed, the coop was empty except for a few red feathers. This sizeable python, now containing a rather large chicken, had Houdini-like exited the secure coop as effortlessly as it had entered. I immediately contacted one of my reptile-obsessed friends, who assured me that it could not have gotten far. Wayan Manis and I gingerly searched the area but there was not a sign of the offender. We carefully checked every centimeter of the coop and could not find a hole. "Ghost snake," suggested Wayan Manis helpfully.

Maude utterly refused to go back into the coop, which undoubtedly vibrated with an unpleasant energetic signature from the previous night's tragedy. She was happy enough to putter around the run all day but at bedtime showed immediate distress when I placed her in the coop. So for several nights she slept in the house – not exactly inside the house, but on the porch, in a collapsible metal cage well lined with straw.

I was concerned about her mental health, though. She had lost her long-time companion and was probably suffering from post traumatic stress disorder. Wayan Manis and I decided that she needed a friend. Mildred arrived the next day, tenderly cradled in a cloth bag under Wayan Manis' arm (we do not hang chickens upside down by the feet in this household).

Mildred was the local equivalent of a battery hen. Wayan Manis had bought her from a woman who kept 20 laying hens in a small coop 24/7 and fed them only dry commercial food. So Mildred was horrified to find herself standing all alone in a roomy pen. She hid under a bush, motionless, for the whole day, clearly suffering from a severe case of agoraphobia. Also she didn't recognize fresh corn, papaya and brown rice as food.

Now I had two traumatized hens. It occurred to me that although I had a short shelf of books on dog, cat and parrot behavior I had never seen a manual on how chickens think. Fortunately, Ubud teems with retired psychologists and I consulted a couple of them, but there did not seem to be any appropriate non-verbal therapies for hens. Your chicken, unlike your parrot, is not a thinking bird. "You have to have a mind before you can lose it," one of these mental health professionals pointed out. "Cuddles and Rescue Remedy," suggested another. "Maybe a little powdered Valium in the food," Margie recommended.

Nyoman dismantled the scene of the crime (the old coop) and fashioned another from strong metal mesh. This one had a floor as well and we reckoned it to be absolutely and completely snake-proof. But when we put the hens into it together, Maude began to peck at poor Mildred, already neurotic, to whom she had taken a dislike. For Mildred's protection, the hens had to take turns being shut up in the coop during the day while the other put in her scratching time in the pen. Maude was still sleeping on the porch.

Our lives were becoming so complicated moving around hens like chess pieces that we decided to let Mildred live in the new coop, move Maude's cage next to it and make two separate pens so they couldn't fight. This worked for a couple of days until one of them figured out how to break into the other pen. Soon they were peaceably scratching together in the straw. Things are back to normal now. Mildred has learned to love taking dust baths and making deep nests in the fragrant rice straw. She eats real food and occasionally presents us with an egg. Maude is back to her bossy self and cranks out an egg daily.

But a python that size requires feeding every two or three weeks and it's getting to be that time again…

Mildred's Last Egg

Spike, the rooster next door, continued to visit the hens frequently to demonstrate his approval, which resulted in plentiful eggs and much loud, competitive beating of wings and crowing to announce all the testosterone coming over the wall.

Then one day I went out at dawn to feed the hens as usual and only Maude ran to meet me. I found Mildred lying in a puddle of feathers in a corner of the pen. She was still warm but very dead, with a nasty, bloody wound on her head. I went off to have a cup of tea and a think. It seemed unlikely to be suicide, although she appeared to have dashed her silly head against a big stone. Then I remembered my little flock of ducks several years ago, all of which had been murdered in a single night by a lawak/musang (a civet-like animal) which had torn their heads off and left them like that. I can't think of any other animal that kills for sport, except humans.

Ibu Mangku next door opined that a scorpion had nailed Mildred. I pointed out that scorpion stings did not cause bleeding in humans but she assured me smugly that they did in chickens. My language skills did not extend to extensive cross examination, so I waited until Wayan Manis arrived. She examined the corpse, and agreed that

Mildred had indeed been dispatched by a musang. This necessitated shutting up the remaining hen (Maude?) at night in a musang-proof enclosure and ordering three more laying hens. They are not easy to obtain and it took a while. Meanwhile Maude followed me around making puzzled noises. Her tiny chicken brain was not a powerful organ, but she was pretty sure there had been more than one of her.

Usually we bury our dead in the garden, but it seemed appropriate somehow that we all share a little of Mildred's energy as she went to the big hen house in the sky. Wayan Manis curried her with ginger, coconut and chilies from the garden. She was a little tough but we agreed that it was nice to all have a piece of her, so to speak. When I left that evening, the dogs were sharing her feet and each parrot was gnawing thoughtfully on one of her drumsticks. She had become one of the family at a molecular level.

When Wayan Manis cleaned her for cooking, she found a little egg factory inside. Eggs are produced in a very businesslike way; no systems analyst could improve on this particular technology. The egg begins inside the hen as one of a string of yellow grains, graduating in size, which will become the egg yolk. When it's large enough, the first yolk on the assembly line enters a passageway where it's fertilized if the hen has been keeping company with a male. (Many otherwise rational people refuse to believe that hens will lay eggs if they are not sharing space with a cock, but they still make eggs whether they are in a relationship or not, just like us. Of course, these eggs won't be fertile.)

The egg will then have the white albumin wrapped around it. Next it moves down the assembly line to the shell-building station. Birds need to have enough calcium in their diet, usually obtained from eating greens, to build healthy shells. When this last step is finished, the egg completes its journey to the outside world. While this is happening, all the other nascent eggs inside are lining up for their turn to be fertilized, albumined and shelled before getting laid. It takes about 24 hours for an egg to go through this whole production cycle. Right after it leaves the factory, the next egg goes onto the assembly line. With Maude's last egg, the one at the top of the assembly line was almost ready to be laid, except the shell was white instead of toasty brown and thinner than usual.

Commercial eggs can never compare with the freshly laid egg of a scratching chicken. The shells are hard, the yolks are deep orange and sit up like little hills. The flavour takes me back to childhood holidays at my grandparent's farm, where soft-boiled eggs in porcelain egg cups were served with sticks of buttered toast (which were called soldiers for some reason) to be dipped in the yolk. It was one of my chores to collect the eggs, which were each dated in pencil and kept in a big blue bowl in the pantry.

Thirty years of accumulated research cracks the myth that eggs are bad for you. When I first wrote about my hens a few months ago and mentioned that my high blood cholesterol meant I should avoid eggs, several readers wrote to me to correct this misconception. Dietary cholesterol has only a small effect on blood cholesterol. Eating eggs does not seem to have any measurable effect on heart disease risk in healthy people. The American Medical Journal recently reported a study that showed no relationship between egg consumption and cardiovascular disease in a population of over 117,000 nurses and health professionals followed for between 8 and 14 years. The study found no difference in the incidence of congestive heart disease or stroke in people eating less than one egg a week and more than one egg a day, except in diabetics.

The American Heart Association recommends one egg a day for adults. And a recent interview with heart specialist Dr Oz revealed that he himself cannot predict which of his bacon, steak and cheese consuming patients will have heart attacks. So I am enjoying my fresh-laid eggs, as are the parrots who get a bit of hard-boiled egg every day.

Maude still produces a warm brown egg every day. She has taken to following the humans around obsessively and the new laying hens have still not arrived. When they do, I will not be naming them. Please remind me.

Along Came a Spider

Arachnophobia, or fear of spiders, may be one of the most widespread phobias in the western world. It's taken me most of my life to become comfortable with these leggy creatures. I grew up in Vancouver, Canada which is not a place one usually associates with arachnids. But we have some monsters there, I assure you, and they bite. Big, dark and hairy, they would scuttle along the floor or wall on dim winter evenings. Tucked up with a book, I would often wonder nervously whether it was a mouse or a spider that had just disturbed my peripheral vision. Sometimes I'd wake up with a swollen bite on my face or arm where a bad-tempered specimen had sunk her fangs while I slept. We called them wolf spiders and many people, even big strong guys, were horrified to find them in the house.

Of course, Australians consider Canadians to be total wimps in the spider department. Their spider population boasts a number of really venomous species, some of which can fell a healthy adult. The Funnel Web spider is indigenous to Sydney, which suggests that it may have been unwise to build a large city on top of a poisonous spider habitat. The males are aggressive and bite with fangs powerful enough to penetrate fingernails and soft shoes. There have been 27 recorded deaths in Australia from spider bites in the past century, 13 from Funnel Web spiders. There is also the Red Back spider and the white tail and mouse spiders, a bite from any of which requires an ambulance ride. There have been no deaths in Australia since the development of an anti-venom but hundreds of people are bitten each year.

A Scottish nun I know who lives part time in a Buddhist nunnery in the Himalayas told me that the worst part of going into retreat for her was the enormous spiders that haunted her cell. How big? She swore that a waste paper basket of normal circumference was inadequate to contain all their legs at once. She told me that when swept off the wall with a broom, the spiders would land on the floor with an audible thud. And when she'd wake in the night and turn on the light there would always be one or two watching her on the wall near her bed, perhaps attracted by her warmth. These gentle giants are harmless, but that doesn't stop them giving us bad dreams.

Of the 35,000 species of spiders described worldwide only a handful are considered to be dangerous, with 27 known to have caused human fatalities. So it's quite a relief to discover that no Balinese spiders are dangerous to humans.

When I decided to write a story about Bali's spiders, I quickly learned that there did not seem to be a single spider expert among my wide and varied acquaintance. After casting my net I learned that Lawrence Lilley, son of Bali-based naturalists Ron and Gayatri Lilley, had spent some time hanging out with an arachnologist from Singapore and he kindly consented to share his knowledge.

Are any of Bali's spiders poisonous? "Actually, all spiders are poisonous to some degree," Lawrence told me. "But very few are poisonous enough to be harmful to humans, and in Indonesia there don't appear to be any lethal spiders. There have been reports of a spider looking like the deadly North American Black Widow or Australian Red Back spider living in dark corners of people's houses here. This is actually the Malabar Spider Nephilengys malabarensis. Its abdomen has a striking orange patch on the underside, making it look superficially like a Black Widow. However, this spider is not dangerous to humans."

One of the most eye-catching spiders in Bali is the Golden Orb web spinner, of the Genus Nephila, named after the large golden web it spins high above the ground. The females have yellow striped or spotted abdomens and long, spindly black legs. Female Golden Orb web spinners can grow very large, with the span of their legs being as wide as a hand. A large fossilized spider, found in China, was a member of the genus Nephila from the Jurassic period.

"The male Orb web spinners are reddish brown or orange and tiny in comparison, probably to avoid being eaten by the female. They are frequently mistaken for baby spiders," Lawrence explained. My staff was shocked and horrified to hear that a female spider will eat her husband (could this be the meaning of consuming passion?) but this is one of the species that do so. Orb web spinners mostly eat the insects they capture in their huge, sticky golden webs and occasionally even small birds. It's amazing to watch a Nephila female, virtually a tiny silk factory, spin and weave the filaments that create a complex metre-wide web in a single night.

These beautiful animals seem to be more common during the rainy season. One wet morning I emerged from my house to find a really giant Nephila trying to climb the stairs into the kitchen. She had lost two of her legs and was pathetically scrabbling to mount the next stair, having somehow managed to navigate several already. Her quest was mysterious; spiders, like other creatures, are basically programmed to seek food and sex and my kitchen could offer her neither. So I gently scooped her up in a saucepan and relocated her to a bush in the garden. But the next morning she was back, trying again to get into the kitchen — what could she be after? It was a long, difficult journey for a handicapped arachnid with no obvious payoff. I finally took her far down to the edge of the jungle and encouraged her to get a life there. When I checked a few days later she had overcome her obsession with my kitchen and spun herself a nice web which had already scored a few juicy bugs, neatly bundled up for future consumption.

"The big brown sawah spiders with fragile legs are probably not spiders at all, but spider relatives called Harvestmen or Daddy Long Legs", Lawrence explained. "Harvestmen have eight legs like spiders, but unlike spiders, which have a clearly defined head (cephalothorax) and abdomen, Harvestmen just have one blob for a body.

I was intrigued (if not exactly thrilled) to learn that there are tarantulas living throughout Indonesia, although seldom reported in Bali. Unlike their giant South American counterparts, Indonesian tarantulas tend to be relatively small. They live in burrows or in tree hollows in a tunnel of webbing, and lay out trip lines radiating from the entrance of their hiding holes. Although their bulky, hairy bodies make them look menacing, they're reluctant to bite and are not lethal to humans.

"Spiders are sold in markets as traditional medicine, and their legs are pulled off to collect 'spider blood' which is also sold as a magic cure-all," reports Lawrence disapprovingly. "It's unfortunate that these practices exist, as spiders are a great help in catching mosquitoes and other pests."

The velvety sawah spiders in Bali are used, according to my housekeeper Wayan Manis, to stop Balinese children from wetting the bed. The spiders are carefully roasted beside an open fire (this is the correct way to cook them, it seems, or else the meat will vapourize; only a fool would fry a spider) before being fed to the child. Apparently one dose is sufficient and the children do not object.

I didn't care how many times I was told that most spiders were harmless, good for the environment and an integral part of the ecosystem. For most of my life they have given me the creeps. I'm ashamed to confess how many innocent arachnids went to an untimely higher rebirth because of me.

Then one dark and stormy night I was driving down that steep, twisty, narrow, dark bit of road between Penestanan and Campuhan. Just at the top, as I was shifting into low gear, I realized that a large spider was shakily navigating the windscreen *inside* the glass very close to my face and hands.

All the clichés I'd ever read about phobias immediately manifested. My blood chilled in my veins, my hair stood straight up on my head and I was having trouble breathing — just as I started the tricky descent. There was nowhere to stop and jump out of the car while making shameful noises, as I'd been known to do in the past. In the grip of my phobia, I had to keep the car on the road while watching the long hairy legs shakily crossing the glass and praying that the hapless creature would not end up in my lap.

That drive was a breakthrough. By the time I arrived home, hyperventilating and drenched in cold sweat, my lifelong terror of spiders was behind me. My heart no longer races when I see one. I admire their engineering and grace. I can go calmly to sleep knowing there is a spider in the bedroom, and casually rake spider webs out of my hair with my fingers as I wander around the garden in early morning. Bali's spiders are safe with me.

Losing the Plot in Paradise

More and more retirees move to Bali every day with the intention of staying here until the end. Some of us will develop dementia. Statistically, the incidence of Alzheimer's Disease (AD) is rising fast everywhere because we're living longer. In the United States over five million people have AD, in Australia about 320,000 and the United Kingdom 820,000. One in 20 Canadians over age 65 is affected by AD. This is not just a disease for westerners. There were 9.19 million people with dementia in China in 2010, up from 3.68 million people in 1990. Worldwide, it's estimated that about 44 million people suffer from Alzheimer's and that will double by 2050.

So some of us living here are definitely going to be losing the plot.

Alzheimer's is an irreversible, progressive brain disease with symptoms that include memory loss, mood changes, problems with communication and reasoning and other issues. One in three seniors in the west die with dementia. There's no single test that can show whether a person has Alzheimer's. While physicians can almost always determine if a person has dementia, it may be difficult to determine the exact cause. Diagnosing Alzheimer's requires careful medical evaluation.

Both early onset AD and late onset AD (after 60) have a genetic component. A person with a direct relative (parent or sibling) with AD has a three times greater chance of developing the disease than someone who does not. The risk increases further if both parents have the disease. Scientists have found genes that can raise people's risk of developing the disease, but they're also looking for other factors that determine who gets the disease and who doesn't. Twice as many women get AD as men. Most researchers no longer regard aluminum as a risk factor for Alzheimer's Disease. Lifestyle plays a part; it's estimated that up to half the cases of AD may be the result of seven key modifiable risk factors: diabetes, high blood pressure, obesity, smoking, depression, cognitive inactivity/low educational attainment, and physical inactivity.

Whatever causes it, it's pointless to obsess about whether you're going to get it or not. Yes, we all forget where we put our keys and the names of people we rarely see, but that's considered normal aging. AD symptoms include memory loss that disrupts daily life, struggling to follow conversations or work with numbers, repeating oneself, trouble reasoning, anxiety, depression, paranoia, getting lost in familiar environments, a declining ability to read, write or speak… check it all out on the Alzheimer's Society website http://www.alz.org

I talked to Susan, who has lived in Bali with her husband Bob for 25 years. About 14 years ago he began to show symptoms of AD, which had killed his mother and aunt. Susan watched her beloved husband slip away from her day by day over the years. "First I noticed that he was getting lost while driving to familiar places. We travelled a lot, and when he packed his bag it would be full of shoes — no shirts. He became angry and frustrated." Then he started hiding things, wandering off and behaving inappropriately. He required constant monitoring. Caring for an Alzheimer's patient is not for the faint of heart.

"After eight years of caring for Bob, I needed help. With assistance from the Bali Advertiser I not only found two caregivers, Nano and

Ketut, but two Australian experts in the field to train us all. This was a godsend. The caregivers and trainers helped immensely by giving me badly needed respite time. Soon Nano and Ketut were sleeping in the house with Bob while I slept in a little room I'd built in the garden."

As the disease progressed and managing Bob became more challenging, the caregivers spent more time with him. They soon invented what they called 'tricks' to keep Bob from harm. Becoming masters of redirecting, they would call after Bob who was about to go walkabout, "Bob, there's a cookie for you in the kitchen." He'd turn around, torn between the urge to go 'somewhere' and satisfying his sweet tooth. By the time he got back to the house he'd forgotten about both his journey and the cookie.

With Alzheimer's the person can't articulate what they feel or where they are. The carers learned to see the signs when Bob needed the bathroom and would get him there before it was too late. They learned how to talk with Bob and draw him out using memories from his childhood.

"Bob was becoming increasingly disruptive at our home-based business," Susan told me. "Miraculously a small cottage became available and the caregivers agreed to try and look after him full time. They hired two other men who they trained and soon we had a team of four dedicated carers. Bob had a dog, a garden and his buddies. They took him on drives to the beach, on walks in the rice paddies, to the gym, for strolls in the village and to meet me for dinners in town. I sent over his favourite foods every day. For someone with severe dementia who couldn't be left alone, he was very happy."

I asked whether she thought we were better off staying in Bali or returning to our own countries if we developed AD. "It's an individual decision," Susan said. "I checked out one place in the US and decided I couldn't do that to him. It was very nice but the confinement, routine and limited outings would have made him even crazier. In Ubud he had a great life."

After several years Bob's disease moved into its final stages. Now the care givers had to deal with total incontinence. When Bob could no longer walk they lifted and shifted him to avoid bed sores.

They spoon-fed him, wheeled him through the village or lifted him into the car for rides so he wouldn't be bored.

"Bob died in March after 14 years of this terrible disease," Susan told me. "I'm so grateful to these men who became his friends and made it possible for him to stay in his beloved Bali and not be stuck in an institution far from me. Because he was close by, I could oversee his care. I can vouch for the carers' abilities. They are not nurses but they're very good caregivers. And whenever we needed medical services, the clinic in Ubud made house calls or sent their ambulance. It was a team effort to give Bob the best life he could have with Alzheimer's. Bob always knew who I was and always kept his sense of humor. He even waited until I returned from a business trip so I could say good-bye before he died three days later."

Gerontology and dementia are not much studied in medical schools in Bali. At the beginning of Bob's journey with Alzheimer's, the doctors and nurses at the clinic in Ubud had no idea how to manage him. Neither did Susan. Over the years, they learned together.

Balinese doctors are more comfortable when foreigners die in a hospital. If we choose to die at home, that decision needs to be discussed in advance, and the banjar and your consulate should be informed.

Bob's carers are now working as drivers and gardeners, which seems like an enormous waste of skill. Two of them also have experience providing compassionate home care to patients with advanced Parkinson's disease, and people immobilized by illness or surgery. Three of them can drive and they all speak some English. They would like to continue care giving, and we can't afford to lose these guys. We're going to need them. Watching a loved slip away from you is terribly hard. Susan shares her journey with Bob in her funny, informative and deeply moving book 'Piece by Piece – Love in the Land of Alzheimer's' available on Kindle.

The Last Lap

One of the big issues for aging expats is the management of our even more aged parents in our original countries.

Every time we leave them to return to our Bali homes we imagine that this might be the last time we see them, knowing that it's a very big world and in an emergency we may not be able to get back in time. Their care often devolves on our stay-at-home siblings who have to manage the dramas and the day to day stuff, while we guiltily return at intervals.

It's a journey. A fall, a stroke or heart attack signals that it's time for them to downsize, leave a home they may have lived in for decades and adjust to an apartment or independent living in a care facility. Some places now have graduated care, where elders first move into an independent apartment where meals and oversight are provided and medical care available when needed. Then they move to a different wing or floor for the Last Lap.

My parents began this journey about six years ago after papa's stroke, first moving from their home of 55 years to an independent living apartment. Six months later they fled the quiet formality of it and found their own unsupervised apartment. Here they forgot to take their meds or cook dinner, causing their daughters to wring their collective hands in despair. Two years later papa, who is legally blind and falls down a lot, went into a care facility nearby. Mama stubbornly clung to her apartment until a month ago.

At last, within sight of her 96th birthday, she conceded that it was time she moved out of her apartment and into an independent living facility near my sister if her cat could go too. British Columbia is enormous so everything is far away; Beth lives on Vancouver Island. She is a star. For years every time there was some medical drama she would board the pets, drive for hours, take a ferry and drive some more to pick up the parents and dust them off, pay the bills, arrange appointments and stock the fridge before making the same journey in reverse.

Every move has been a major drama. My God, the stuff they collected. Mama has Obsessive Compulsive Disorder, one symptom of which is hoarding. Papa was just a hoarder. Emptying their house was a lengthy nightmare, as they refused to admit that the contents of an overfurnished four bedroom home were not going to fit into a small apartment.

After the second move mama managed to completely jam her apartment full of unnecessary objects. Any bare, flat surface was an anathema to her and she was deeply attached to every piece of paper and ornament. Just opening the subject of downsizing her collection of artificial flowers started a tantrum. We went slowly, packing maybe one box a day.

This would clearly take forever, and after delivering a box to the op shop I came home to discover she had – guess what? – brought home more stuff. This was hard on my blood pressure. Hers was fine.

One day we went through a thick folder of recipes carefully clipped from newspapers and magazines, the most recent of which was dated 1974. This is a woman who hated to cook, but there was no possibility of just heaving out the file. Every single recipe had to be unfolded, read aloud and its merits discussed. I did manage to reduce the collection to a small envelope of things she has never cooked and never will. That's not the point. It's a control issue. The Last Lap means having to give up most of the material possessions acquired over a lifetime as territory shrinks from a house to an apartment to a single room. Mama guards her stuff fiercely.

The next morning we tackled the rock collection. A few years ago she began to pick up interesting rocks: beach agates, river stones with ribbons of minerals in them, fossils. It's amazing what mama can see with her solitary, ancient eye (she lost the other one about 50 years ago). She consented to curate her collection and selected a few favourites so I could release the rest back into the wild. This took hours.

"I think I need a calming-down pill," she said faintly when I opened the door of the locker in the basement. Among the empty suitcases, unlabeled boxes and patio furniture were about 6,000 photographic slides spanning the family's history over 60 years. The thought of reviewing these sent us back upstairs where we shared a calming-down pill and a pot of tea. This Last Lap is not for sissies, and many of us are not exactly spring chickens ourselves. Downsizing for the Last Lap is physically heavy, highly emotional work and it goes on for a long time.

A few weeks later papa passed away peacefully, Beth and I on each side of the bed holding his hands. A month after that mama was established in her new apartment in a care facility near Beth's house on Vancouver Island, along with her cat and much of her stuff. She has started collecting rocks again.

In Indonesia I believe geriatrics is not even offered as a specialty. So there's very little informed support when coping with a partner or parent with dementia, a condition very common with advancing age. My Balinese neighbours have their hands full with two elders in the compound who have dementia. There are no calming-down pills here, it seems.

We have very few rites of passage in our culture, compared to the Balinese who acknowledge so many nuances of life. Ours are Spartan indeed by comparison: birth, perhaps a graduation, marriage, (long pause) death. Like menopause, that other unacknowledged rite of passage, the Last Lap is not a single event but a process that goes on for years. The Last Lap with a parent is seldom easy. Beth and I try to see it as an ongoing sitcom with an aging cast and unpredictable script.

Our own Last Laps are usually of unknown duration. Here in Bali we are blessed to have the choice of where the play will run its course, and with whom. There's a lot of dark humour there if you dig for it. Get out your shovel.

Made in the USA
Columbia, SC
06 November 2018